THE GUANCHES
SURVIVORS
AND THEIR DESCENDANTS

José Luis Concepción

First Edition, November, 1984

Twenty-second Edition: April, 2018

© José Luis Concepción
(Ediciones Graficolor)
©Editorial M. E. Lorenzo Rodríguez
Calle El Charcón, 39
38320 La Laguna, Tenerife
Islas Canarias
Tel-fax: 922646273
ediciones graficolor@hotmail.com

Depósito Legal: TF 292-2010
I.S.B.N.: 84-920527-5-9

Original Title: "Los guanches que sobrevivieron
y su descendencia"

to my children, Armide and Benayga

CONTENTS

INTRODUCTION

The history of the conquest and colonization of the Canary Islands and, in particular, the more populous amongst them, was suitably manipulated by the colonizers and their descendants over a long period and certain stories have endured until the present day, all of which has somewhat masked the reality of the events. This can be seen in the writings of Viana, who invented everything that came to mind as he elaborated on his fanciful poetry. This author enjoyed the following of a faithful few who, referring to Lugo, used such patriotic terms as «our general» and «our people» and devoted themselves to concealing the barbarous activities of the conquerors. The phrases themselves have no particular meaning, the most significant fact about these historians is their eagerness to praise the names of the men who conquered the islands, nearly always, their attitude towards the indigenous islanders whom they held in contempt and humiliated. Proof of this is the negligible amount of trouble they took to record so many important matters about which we now know nothing.

I hope to demonstrate by means of this book that the Guanche race did not in fact disappear, as many people believe. Their language has disappeared, as well as their culture and socio-political system, but the people have remained and that is the most important thing. It is not the purpose of this book to establish who has more Guanche blood or less Guanche blood.

The majority of Canary Islanders know little or practically nothing at all about the Guanches and it seems to me that ordinary people have not been made sufficiently aware of our history since it has been published almost always in bulky volumes and collections. I have seen, too, that even though many families may own books on Canary history, they never get around to reading them for, as we all know, few people nowadays can afford to spend much time reading.

Not only is this a collection of the most important aspects of our history, albeit in abridged form, but is is a book which anyone can read through in a short time to acquire a knowledge of some of the basic facts. People wishing to go more deeply into our history can do so by referring to the bibliography of works used in compiling this book.

In the first section of this book there is a brief study of the origins of the Guanches and their customs for people unaware of them, since I consider a knowledge of these to be of fundamental importance, and this serves as the basis of a chapter entitled «Guanche Survival».

In the second section I have limited myself to referring to the most important events of the conquest with particular regard to the number of deaths that took place.

And lastly, in the third section, with as little commentary as possible, I have recorded the numerous documents which have been found in connectionwith the Guanches and such important events as the removal of various governors; the trials of Lugo and the lady Bobadilla who were obliged to make compensation to some of the native people for maltreatment; the motives which compelled the Guanches to deny their own race... and finally I have enumerated the Guanche customs which have survived until the present day.

FIRST SECTION

THE ORIGINS AND WAY OF LIFE OF THE GUANCHES

WHAT WERE THE GUANCHES LIKE?

We al know that the Guanches were the ancient settlers of the Canary Islands, although this has resulted in a certain amount of confusion since it is understood that the Guanches only existed in Tenerife. Certainly, the inhabitants of Tenerife were known as Guanches and when the colonists first arrived the people of the different islands were defined as Guanches, Canarios, Gomeros, Palmeros. But given the common origin of the islands' indigenous inhabitants, for quite a long time now the word «Guanche» has been used to cover them all.

They were not the giants many people imagine them to be, being neither particularly tall nor heavily-built. Obviously there were some rather tall people amongst them but the large majority were of medium build[1]. In fact, it has been scientifically proved that they were of medium build, although the Gomeros tended to be smaller than the inhabitants of Tenerife and the inhabitants of Fuerteventura relatively taller[2].

There existed two different races, basically: the Cro-Magnon and the Mediterranean. According to Dr. Ilse Schwidetzky, the Cro-Magnon type is recognized by his strong-featured, broad face and long, narrow skull, and the Mediterranean type by its long, delicately-featured face and short, broad skull[3].

There was no communication between the Guanches of the different islands because they possessed no knowledge of navigation. They were a peaceful people with high, moral standards, very courageous and great defenders of the liberty of their homeland. Noble, compassionate and true to their word.

After the arrival of Jean Bethencourt, his priests wrote: «Go throughout the world and nowhere will you find a finer and better-formed people than those who inhabit these islands, both men and women, with great minds were they to receive instruction»[4].

11

POLITICAL AND SOCIAL STRUCTURE

At the time of the conquest, the Canary Islands were ruled by one or various kings or princes on each island. In Gran Canaria the king was known as GUANARTEME and in Tenerife as MENCEY. Each king had his own counsellors or chiefs. In Tenerife, for instance, there were three distinct social levels: the ACHIMENCEYES, holding the rank next to mencey, ACHICIQUITZA, the nobility, and ACHICAXNA, peasant. The chief or counsellor was the SIGOÑE.

In Gran Canaria the high priest was known as FAYCAN, the counsellor or chief as GUAIRE or GAIRE and the judge as FAYACAN. Upon his nomination the mencey had to take the following oath: «Agoñe Yacoron Yñatsahña Chacoñamet»[5], I swear by the bone of him who made me great. This ceremony was conducted in the «tagoror».

Laws differed on each island: in El Hierro, the person who committed a robbery for the first time had his eye put out and the second time, his other eye.

In Gran Canaria murderers were put to death and robbers were imprisoned.

In Fuerteventura criminals had their heads crushed by a rock.

In Tenerife the death penalty did not exist. Thieves were punished severely, and a lack of respect towards women led to some particularly severe punishment. A murderer had all his belongings taken away from him to be given as compensation to the victim's family and was banished from the kingdom.

In La Palma theft went unpunished since it was considered to be an art.

Each king met with his counsellors in the tagoror (a circular open space made of stone) to deal with the various matters at hand and administer justice.

Any man could become a noble. He was judged by his personal merits and lack of bad habits. In the ceremony it was asked if he had been seen killing or milking goats or preparing food with this own hands, if he had been a thief in times of peace or had acted improperly, especially towards a woman. If the reply was in the negative, he was created a noble, however if the reply was positive, his hair was cropped and he remained forever a peasant with the nickname of the cropped one.

WORK AND HANDICRAFTS

The Guanches devoted themselves mostly to herding but also to agriculture. They grew cereals, using goats' horns for digging the earth and the women used to help them to sow barley, wheat and beans by dropping the seeds into the ground. They also knew how to put to use the running water to cultivate the land.

They made pottery and were quite good at decorating it. They made a variety of containers in different colours and sizes. «They would make them by hand and coat them with red ochre and once these were dry they would burnish them with smooth stones and they would become very lustrous and durable. They would make them large and small, cups and dishes...»[6].

TYPES OF DWELLINGS

They lived mainly in caves and, where there were none, in huts. In Gran Canaria, where more advanced civilizations had reached the island, they used to build houses made of stone and lived in what, virtually, were villages. Their beds were made of dried grasses and they used skins to wrap up in.

CLOTHING AND ADORNMENTS

They dressed in garments (tamarcos) made of soft goat or sheep-skins which were generally well made. In Gran Canaria they also wore skirts made of well-woven rushes or palm fronds. According to Torriani, the garments the women wore were made of treated skins like those used in Lombardy and other places. «... they were covered from the neck to the feet. They plaited their hair with rushes instead of ribbons and let it fall freely over their shoulders, leaving their foreheads uncovered as the prime focus of their beauty»[7]. Father Espinosa said that «... they called this sort of apparel tamarco and it was common to men and women; except that the women for the sake of decency wore beneath the tamarco something like an underslip of soft skin..., because it was improper for women to reveal breasts and feet»[8].

Their footwear was made of skins as well, known in Tenerife as xercos and maho in Lanzarote and Fuerteventura.

They were adorned with necklaces made of clay beads, sea-shells, pebbles and bone.

Natives of Gran Canaria.

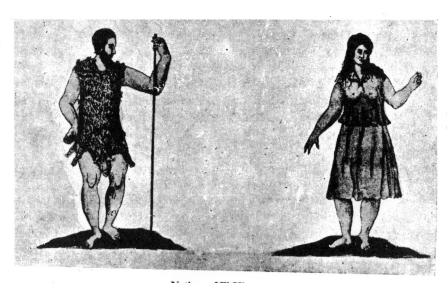

Natives of El Hierro.

Torriani, pp. 107 and 115, «Descripción de las Islas Canarias», Ediciones Goya, Santa Cruz de Tenerife, 1978.

14

FOOD

The only animals they raised were goats, sheep, pigs and dogs. They would use the goats and sheep for their milk, from which they made cheese and lard, and eat their meat; they also ate pig-meat[9], although some chroniclers have claimed that pigs were considered to be sacred animals.

They made **gofio** by using stone mills to grind barley, wheat and beans into meal which they then roasted in a type of clay oven. They ate fruit, including figs, molasses tapped from trees, seafood, dates, flour made from fern-roots and fish which they would catch in rush or palm-from nets or with goat-horn hooks.

TOOLS AND ARMS

In the home, in addition to the usual pottery implements, they used mills, wooden bowls and combs, pouches made from kids' stomachs (baifo), leather bags to carry things in, bags made of rushes (carianas) in Gran Canaria, knives carved from obsidian, needles made from fish-bones or bodkins fashioned from bone for sewing the skins together.

The herdsmen would use very long, well-smoothed poles for vaulting gullies and steep rocks bit and sometimes they also used short rods.

They armed themselves with a **banot** (similar to a javelin) in Tenerife, a **magado** in Gran Canaria, a **moca** in La Palma, and **tezzeses** in Fuerteventura as well as other wooden weapons. And they were also armed with tabonas (cutting stones) which were the first weapon they used in conflict.

FESTIVITIES AND SPORTS

The main festivity was the beñesmen which used to be held after the cereals and fruit were harvested in the summer. This particular festivity consisted of various turns: the **guatativoa** feast, dancing and singing, contests or challenges involving stone-lifting, wrestling, the pole game and so on. «They would in the year (which they counted by lunations) assemble together on many occasions; and the king who ruled at that time would offer them meats, gofio, milk and lard, ... and here each one would display his valour and give thanks by making a show of leaping, running, dancing, wrestling and other things they could contrive»[10].

In Fuerteventura they competed by using their poles to spring high. Another challenge demanding a display of courage involved placing objects on highly dangerous cliff-edges[11].

If they were at war, it was the custom to declare a truce when the festivities began.

SONGS AND DANCES

The Guanches were fond of singing and dancing. «They had a place where they would gather to dance and sing. Their dancing was dainty and refined, the same dance that is now called «The Canary». Their songs were sorrowful and sad, or tender, or funereal, and which they called dirges»[12]. This latter was to become a famous dance in Europe. «It is a dance of request and rebuff, in which two rows of dancers face one another in pairs, they draw close and away again with graceful leaps and taps, some of truly difficult»[13].

MARRIAGE

All that was needed to constitute marriage was the consent of the two partners, and it could be dissolved if so desired by either partner. The inconvenient aspect about this, however, was that the children of this union were regarded as illegitimate and not belonging to the new union. Abreu Galindo wrote, «... the Canarios did not marry more than one woman, even though the aforementioned writers say otherwise. neither is it certain that pregnant women were put into the temples, nor that after giving birth they were separated from their husbands and allowed to buy a slave to satisfy and appease their appetite... because in these islands it was not known what slaves were...»[14].

LANGUAGE AND INSCRIPTIONS

The language spoken by the Guanches on the various islands had a common origin but with, it seems, differences of dialect. Certain words were the same on all the islands, such as AHEMEN or AHEMON, water; AHO, milk; GANIGO, clay vessel; GOFIO, **roasted meal**; MOCAN, a tree; TABONA, cutting stone; TAMARCO, garment; VERODE, a plant... and many other words. Speech was very soft, noted the chroniclers.

Several inscriptions have been found engraved in hard rocks on various islands; in La Palma can be found lots of spiral shapes, and in El Hierro, circles with crosses in the middle and other signs. The inscriptions in Gran Canaria are similar to those found in El Hierro and the rocks are painted, too; Lanzarote is another island which has engraved rocks resembling those of La Palma.

RELIGION

According to Abreu Galindo and Espinosa, the primitive peoples believed in a supreme being whom they called by «ABORAC» or «ACORAN» amongst other names. However certain chroniclers have written that they believed in demons such as the **guayota,** who lived in the volcano of Teide (echeide or hell); but the fact that they believed in the existence of hell does not mean that they did not believe in God.

Each tribe had its own priests and temples or places of worship. In Gran Canaria there lived a type of priestess (**harimaguadas**) whose sole duty was that of prayer and instruction. Their convents were called **tamogantes** and the temple **almogaren**[15].

In Tenerife they used to separate the lambs from the sheep and then use their bleating together with prayer to implore God to send rain.

Other, similar, rites took place on the other islands and food was also offered to God.

Speaking about Tenerife, Father Espinosa said, «... It is plain and clear to see that the natives of this island (not excepting those of the other islands...) were noble uncontaminated, with no rites, ceremonies, sacrifices nor adoration of fictitious gods nor dealing nor conversation with demons as in other nations... and with a perfect understanding of God»[16].

EMBALMINGS AND BURIALS

In the Canary Islands as in ancient Egypt and Peru, the dead were embalmed. Some mummies have been preserved and can be seen in the Canary Museum in Las Palmas and the Archaeological Museum in Santa Cruz de Tenerife.

Espinosa tells us that the mummification process consisted of first washing the body; then after this a liquid made up of melted animal, lard, heather and rock dust, pine bark and herbs was inserted into the body through the mouth. They treated the cadaver in this way for fifteen days whilst it was drying out in the sun. Then they wrapped it in skins and left it on a block of **tea** wood in a funeral cave. It was then given the name of **xaxo.**

Others, though, were simply buried in caves, and in the north-west of Gran Canaria there lived people who buried their dead in tumulus.

As you will appreciate, despite a lack of communication between the islands, generally speaking, the way of life owing to a common origin ·adapted, though, to the varying conditions on each island. The mode of dress, the grinding stones, the language, the way the various peoples were ruled, in fact many customs were similar from island to island.

THE TUMULUS

Agaete, Gran Canaria: aboriginburriels in «Los Cascajos», Camino de los Molinos, Las Nieves.

Description given by Sebastian Sosa Barroso. These tumulus were destroyed and covered with earth, in the decade of the forties of this century, to plant bananas.

THE ORIGIN OF THE GUANCHES

Since the discovery and conquest of the Canary Archipelago, the origins of the Guanches have intrigued many historians and researchers.

Until relatively recently, several different theories had evolved which included such possibilities as their being of Viking origin, or Greek or Roman, Phoenecian, Carthaginian, Egyptian or Libyan.

Since the discovery of human remains (Cro-Magnon) in South-West France in 1968 and later, similar findings in North-West Africa (in Morocco, Algeria and Tunisia), matters have somewhat become clearer. The type of burial involved demonstrates that either the Cro-Magnon types of North Africa were descended from the French Cro-Magnons, or were two closely-matched peoples.

The Cro-Magnon of the Canaries also buried his dead in the same way as the peoples mentioned above.

Taking this into account, plus the language, customs, food and features of the Berbers, it seems natural to conclude that the Guanches really did travel from the area of Barbary and ancient Libya, since the language spoken by the Guanches had certain Libyan roots.

It is still not known how they reached the Canary Islands, although if we take into consideration the marine currents flowing from Africa to the Canaries we can suppose that they arrived in some sort of rudimentary crafts.

Speaking of La Palma, Abreu Galindo said, «they were ruled and governed by chiefs as were the Africans»[17]. And referring to Gran Canaria he said, «whencever they came, it is most likely to be true that the first to arrive on these islands of Canaria came from Africa... I am also made to think that they have come from Africa by the many words the natives of these islands have in common with the people of the three nations in those African parts which are Berber and Azaneg and Alarab. Because Telde which is the oldest village on this island of Canaria, and Gomera and Orotava in Tenerife, are names which are found in the kingdom of Tez and Benamarín. And on the Cape of Aguer are some cultivated areas they call the gardens of Telde»[18].

Dealing with the origins of the Guanches, Espinosa said, «Of these opinions the reader may choose that which he thinks apt yet I shall insist that in my opinion they are African and that from there they are descended, by virtue of the proximity of the lands and the closeness of their customs and tongue, whichever part they come from. Add to this as well that the food is the same, such as gofio, milk, lard etc.»[19].

It must be stated here that the Berber tribes are not Arabs; they can be either fair or dark-haired, with white skin, who settled in that region thousands of years ago and in centuries past were invaded by the Arabs but still keep the same customs and language.

The following is a list I have compiled of comparisons of Berber and Guanche names, from the book by Sabino Berthelot:

ADEJE, valley, district, small town in Tenerife.
ADEJAD, Berber tribe in Morocco.

AGULO, village in La Gomera.
AGULU, «Cabil» tribe and village in Morocco.

TABORNO, valley and village in mountains in Nort-West of Tenerife.
TABORNOST, village in Morocco, situated at 30°0' and 8°35°24» long. D.E.

TAGARAGRE, mountainous area in La Palma (Barlovento).
TAGGARAYIA, mountain in Marocco situated at 31°20' lat. and 9°40'.

TASO, mountain on island of La Gomera.
TASA, Berber village in Morocco.

TEGUISE, village in Lanzarote.
TEGHASAH, village in Morocco.

TELDE, village in Gran Canaria in a fertile part of the island.
TEDLAH, Province of Morocco located in a highly fertile region.

TEMESEN, arid plain and village in Fuerteventura.

THEMSNA, expression used in the dialect of Gadanes, meaning arid areas and deserts.

VOCABULARY

AHEMON, water. L. H.
AHO, milk. L. C.
ALMOGAREN, the holy place. G.C.
CARIANA, basket. G.C.
BENAHOARE, name of the island of La Palma.
GOMERA, name of the island of La Gomera.
TAGINASTE, a tree (bush). C.
TAHUYEN, «gupe». G.
TEMASEN, barley. L.
TIGOT, sky. P.
TIGOTAN, skies. P.

AMON, in Schilah.
AGCHO or AGHO, idem.
TALMOGAREN, idem.
CARIAN, idem.
BENI HAOURAH, Berber tribe.
GHOMERAH, Berber tribe.
TAGINOST, a palm branch. (Schil.)
TAHUYOT, coverlet or cloak. (Schil.)
TOMZEN, in Schilah.
TIGOT, in Schilah.
TIGOTAN, in Schilah.

Other words are provided by RITTER, although some correspond to those provided by GLAS, JACKSON and VATER.

TAGOROR: counselling place. T.
AHOREN: barley flour. T.
AZAMOTAN: kneaded barley. L.
TIHAXA: sheep.

TAGARER: place of punishment (Berber)
AHOREN: barley flour (Berber)
AZAMOTAN: kneaded barley (Berber)
THIKHSI: sheep (Berber)[20].

Many parallels exist between the Libyan-Berber peoples and the Guanches and there are still Berbers today who lead a life similar to that of the primitive inhabitants of the Canaries. «The North of Africa presents ample proof of these dwellings in present times, without the necessity of taking us back to prehistoric ages, if we compare this form of life with the so-called culture of the Nort African caves... The household wares found in this type of dwelling are extremely poor and intimately related to food: the mill, some dishes and pots for the preparation of food»[21]. Another tradition is the method of working with ceramics: «... this is found extensively throughout North Africa from Jarjar in the South of Tunisia, to the Central Atlas. We perceive that this technique has survived until the present day, both in the islands and in the African zone cited»[22].

SECOND SECTION

CONQUEST OF THE CANARY ISLANDS

THE CONQUEST OF LANZAROTE

Until 1402, apart from raids and exploratory missions in the course of which some of the indigenous inhabitants were taken captive, these islands did not undergo any notable changes.

In this year, a Norman baron, Juan de Bethencourt, accompanied by his lieutenant Gadifer de la Salle, the priests Jean de Verrier and Pierre Bontier, and with a few soldiers, arrived at Lanzarote. With them were the interpreters Isabel and Fernando who had been captured locally some years earlier. As the party disembarked, the islanders hid in the mountains.

This island was called «TITEROYUGATRA»[23] and was ruled by one king by the name of Guadarfía.

Once the Europeans had disembarked, the natives of Lanzarote approched respectfully and admiringly. The Europeans spoke of friendship, and mindful of the plundering the island had suffered in recent years the king granted them permission to stay there and build a castle and he made all his people available to Jean de Bethencourt. This could be seen as a pact of friendship on the part of Guardafía.

Once the Europeans were established in Lanzarote they made a reconnaissance trip to Fuerteventura and in the meantime, Bethencourt, who was in the service of the Spanish Crown, left for Spain to seek reinforcements for resuming the conquest.

During his absence some serious incidents took place. Whilst Gadifer was on the islet of Lobos collecting seals, a rebellion broke out headed by Bertin de Berneval, who captured some natives to sell as slaves and then fled to Spain, leaving Gadifer without a boat and on the point of dying of thirst. The islanders of Lanzarote were thus roused to revolt and killed some of the Europeans, most of whom were able to take refuge in the fort.

Gadifer wished to avenge the death of his people and consented to a proposal made by the native, Atchen, that this latter should reveal the whereabouts of the king; Gadifer could then take him prisoner and Atchen seize the crown himself. This was carried out and the native prisoners were released and the king himself imprisoned. Atchen then attacked the Europeans but Guadarfía was able to escape and had the traitor Atchen burned alive. This in turn led to fierce fighting and Gadifer considered the idea of putting all the natives to death but for the women and children. He was dissuaded from this by the priests, however, who hastened to instruct the local people in religion and baptize them, although the latter were then reduced to slavery[24]. Thus the island was conquered and when Bethencourt arrived, had more than three hundred soldiers[25]. Guadarfía surrendered voluntarily with a few men obedient to him and after he had been baptized was allowed to go free and given land as were the other natives.

THE CONQUEST OF FUERTEVENTURA

When Bethencourt returned in 1404 with reinforcements, he wanted to conquer the island of Fuerteventura, where two forts had been built, at Rico Roque and Valtarajal.

Fuerteventura was divided into two kingdoms: Maxorata and Jandía, ruled by Guize and Ayoze respectively.

Several battles took place in which many of the indigenous inhabitants died, and those who were captured were sent to Lanzarote.

Guadarfía took part in the conquest of the island, accompanied by his men from former times.

The natives who had taken refuge in the mountains kept up their resistance, however they finally realized the futility of this and decided to give themselves up.

In January, 1405, Guize surrendered, accompanied by forty of his men and was baptized. Ayoze, too, gave himself up the following day and then the remaining inhabitants followed their example.

The two kings continued to live on the island and received their share of lands.

THE CONQUEST OF EL HIERRO

This island was ruled over by one king, Armiche, and when Bethencourt arrived, Augeron, the king's brother who had been captured in earlier years, acted as interpreter.

Bethencourt assured Armiche he had come in peace but as soon as the king made an appearance he was taken prisoner and it was agreed to divide the land and slaves amongst the hundred and twenty colonists who knew how to cultivate the earth[26].

THE PARTIAL CONQUEST OF LA GOMERA

La Gomera was divided into four kingdoms: Agana, Hipalán, Mulagua and Orone, which were ruled by Alguabozegue, Alhagal, Aberbequeye and Masegue respectively[27].

The first two submitted to Jean de Bethencourt but the other two resisted so strongly that neither Bethencourt nor his nephew, Maciot, could manage to conquer them.

The Gomeros were so brave and so tough that they were only forced to submit pacifically as much as eighty years after the first colonists had arrived. Thus no one really knows who conquered the island because it was never wholly conquered as such.

The conduct of Bethencourt in El Hierro was different from his conduct in Lanzarote and Fuerteventura. After conquering these three islands and when La Gomera had been half conquered, he decided to depart for France, leaving his nephew Maciot in full control.

THE ADMINISTRATION OF MACIOT DE BETHENCOURT, SALES AND TRANSFERS OF THE CANARY ISLANDS

Maciot de Bethencourt was accepted as ruler at the beginning but there soon arose problems with the rebellion of the Hierro slaves in the service of their overlords whose behaviour had become markedly tyrannical; they had organized the capture of natives in Gran Canaria to be sold as slaves and ignored the advice of the Bishop of Rubicón, who was compelled to denounce them to the Crown of Castile.

Consequently, Enrique de Guzmán, Count of Niebla, was ordered by the Crown to transfer possession of the islands to Guillén de las Casas in 1430. Five years later, Fernán Peraza was to inherit them.

At the request of Maciot de Bethencourt, the Portuguese mounted an invasion of Lanzarote but were expelled two years later by the natives.

Fernán Peraza was succeded by the husband of Inés Peraza, Diego Herrera. He divided the domain between his children. Fernán Peraza «the Younger» inherited La Gomera and El Hierro, and Sancho de Herrera, María de Ayala and Constanza de Sarmiento, Lanzarote and Fuerteventura.

THE CONQUEST OF GRAN CANARIA

The year 1477 marked the beginning of the islands' conquest at the command of the Catholic King and Queen of Castile. This was to prove notably different from former conquests.

Three redoubtable islands still had to be conquered. Gran Canaria was the first to be attacked and was one of the islands to offer most resistance to the intending conquerors. In the many years of conflict the Canarios always emerged victorious.

On the arrival of Juan Rejón in 1478, the island was ruled by two kings, or **guanartemes**: Thenesor Semidan in Galdar, the northern zone and Doramas in Telde, the southern zone.

The two guanartemes agreed to join forces and attack the Spanish encampment in Las Palmas which was being fortified.

«There were more than two thousand Canarios very well armed in their manner»[28].

Amongst the most courageous were Doramas, Adargoma and Maninidra. Juan Rejón had sent a messenger to the Canarios to tell them he had come at the request of the King and Queen of Castile to convert them to Christianity. He told them they would be under his protection but that if they did not obey him he would pursue them to the death and convert those remaining into slaves. The Canarios' answer to this was that «another day they would give a reply»[29].

The following day at dawn Doramas decided to attack. In the battle of «Guiniguada», according to A. Galindo, three hundred Canarios lost their lives but only thirty, if we are to believe Gómez Escudero[30]. Adargama was wounded and taken prisoner.

With the passing of the months, the Spaniards continued to fortify the camp, however there were disagreements amongst them as a consequence of the serious situation in which they found themselves. Dean Bermudes notified the King and Queen of this, whereupon Rejón was removed and sent back to Spain when Pedro de Algaba arrived, accompanied by Bishop Frías, to take up the post of governor.

During Algaba's period of governorship, it was decided to make an attack by way of Tirajana on 24th August, 1479.

The natives observed the Spaniards landing along the coast and hid up in the hills. The Spaniards reached the valley where they were hiding without realizing the danger they were in and on their return were attacked unexpectedly. Twenty-six Christians died, more than a hundred were wounded and eighty were taken prisoner[31].

Juan Rejón returned to the island and ordered Pedro de Algaba to be beheaded. As a result of the revenge and outrages committed by Rejón, the King and Queen nominated Pedro de Vera as governor of the island and he arrived in 1480, bringing with him men and horses.

THE DEATH OF DORAMAS

Vera decided that Galdar must be conquered and when he arrived in the northern kingdom he met the courageous Doramas. A fierce battle followed and Vera, thinking that if he were to eliminate Doramas he could win, made his way over accompanied by a group of soldiers. In the ensuing fight, Doramas split open the skull of one Spaniard but Pedro de Vera wounded him in the left side with a lance and Diego de Hozes managed to wound him in the shoulder; Doramas, though, still had enough strength left to break one of Hozes' legs. Finally, Pedro de Vera delivered him a blow in the chest and he died, calling the man who had wounded him in the back a traitor[32].

Following the loss of their leader the Canarios returned to the mountains, leaving behind some men who saw to the burial of Doramas.

THE SECOND ATTACK ON TIRAJANA

Pedro de Vera decided to build a fort in Agaete, with the help of the Canarios who had been conquered or taken captive and when it was completed he left Alonso de Lugo in command with a force of thirty men[33].

The Spaniards launched another attack on Tirajana but the Canarios in their mountain stronghold were able to kill twenty-five of them and injure many more. After a slight advance, the Spaniards decided to withdraw to the camp at Las Palmas, where they were attacked several times by the Canarios, under the leadership of the daring BENTAGAY. One day he arrived at the camp, saying that he wanted to become a Christian, and after he had made a reconnaissance of the fort, he left again and returned by night to kill guards and horses and generally cause as much havoc as possible[34].

THE SUBMISSION OF THE GUANARTEME OF GALDAR

With the aid of Fernán Peraza, Pedro de Vera continued the conquest and was able to surprise the guanarteme, THENESOR SEMIDAN, and fifteen others, including the brave Maninidra, in a cave. Together with their families they gave themselves up and were taken to the Spanish Court, where the guanarteme was baptized with the name of Fernando and brought back to the island to advise the resistants to surrender. But Fernando Guanarteme was unable to persuade them to do so because after they had seen the ill-treatment of those who had become Christians they preferred to continue fighting.

Pedro de Vera attempted to reach the top of one of the mountains where many women and children, but no men, had taken refuge, and after fifteen days, during which time he was unable to achieve their surrender because of the quantities of rocks they showered down on him, he was forced to abandon the site. He had lost eight fighting men and many others were injured[35].

THE FINAL RESISTANCE

The Canarios had taken refuge in their fortified mountain stronghold but this was penetrated by the Spaniards killing some of those who had tried to resist and with the aid of Fernando Guanarteme they could take many others captive. Then the Spaniards went on to the stronghold of AJODAR and Capitain Miguel de Moxica, who wanted to avenge all the deaths and defeats, tried to make the ascent with his men. He lost his life, however, as did most of his followers. Areu Galindo said, «If Pedro de Vera had not brought reinforcements and Fernando de Galdar, whom the Canarios respected, had not come, all would have died here because a contingent of three hundred Canarios came to the aid of their own forces»[36].

Pedro de Vera withdrew to the Las Palmas camp to recuperate and after seeking more men on the islands of Lanzarote, Fuerteventura and La Gomera, was determined to bring the conquest to an end.

«ANSITE», THE LAST STRONGHOLD

One stronghold remained to be taken, between Tirajana and Galdar, and Fernando Guanarteme realizing that his people had taken refuge there with their women and children, begged them to give themselves up and take pity on their dependants, who would otherwise die. The valiant warriors followed the counsel of their former guanarteme, who had assured them they would be well-treated, and laid down their arms amidst shouts and weeping. Chief Bentejuí and the Faycán embraced one another and hurled themselves over the cliff-edge, crying «ATISTIRMA». Two women followed their example[37].

THE CONQUEST OF LA PALMA

The islands of La Palma and Tenerife had yet to be conquered and it was Alonso Fernández de Lugo who took charge of this undertaking after taking part in the conquest of Gran Canaria. He set sail for the mainland and returned with more men and money, to be joined in Gran Canaria by some of the island's conquerors and a fair number of Canarios.

At the time of the conquerors' arrival, La Palma was divided into twelve provinces: ARIDANE, TIHUYA, TAMANCA, AHENGUARE-ME, TIGALATE, TEDOTE, TENEGUA, ADEYAHAMEN, TAGA-RAGRE, TAGALGUEN, HISCAGUAN and ACERO, ruled by, respectively, MAYANTIGO, ECHEDEY, ECHENTIVE and AZUCUA-HE, JARIGUO and GAREAGUA, BENTACAYCE, ATABARA, BE-DIESTA, TEMIABA, BEDIESTA (of Tagalguen), ATOGMATOMA and TANAUSU[38].

The island had come under attack on various occasions but remained unconquered. The most important attempt had been made by Guillén Peraza, the son of Fernán Peraza, but he lost his life along with two hundred of his men[39].

On reaching La Palma, Lugo landed on the beaches of Tazacorte and with the help of the local interpreter, Gazmira la Palmense, who had been taken captive previously, convinced the natives not to put up resistance by making them false promises, and the peoples of Aridane, Tihuya, Tamanca and Ahenguareme duly surrendered. But when he arrived at Tigalate, it was to find the two princes who governed them on a war footing and unwilling to surrender. Lugo fought against them and won, killing some and wounding others, and those who remained fled to the mountains. The conquest continued without too many problems, with most of the local people hiding in the hills. However, when they reached the area of ACERO (Caldera de Taburiente), ruled by the redoubtable TANAUSU, they were unable to get any further. They tried their luck elsewhere but still without success, so they despatched a relation of Tanausu who had been baptized to convince him that he would be well-treated and could remain on his lands if he were to give himself up.

TANAUSU replied that he would speak with Lugo but wished the Christians to withdraw from his territory. But when he approached the meeting-place, trusting in the Spaniards and unheeding of the advice of his relation UGRANFIR that they did not come in peace, he was surprised by Lugo and his troops and fierce fighting ensued, with the loss of men on both sides. «Tanausu was captured, lamenting that Alonso de Lugo had not remained true to his word»[40].

Fernández de Lugo put Tanausu and some other Palmeros on to a ship for Spain, but the valiant leader preferred to die of hunger after losing sight of his land. «VACAGUARE, VACAGUARE», cried Tanausu, «I want to die».

Thus Lugo betrayed a man who, after a just fight for his homeland, had been on the verge of surrender.

THE CONQUEST OF TENERIFE

This fearsome island still remained to be conquered. Many an attempt had been launched by the conquerors from the other islands which had already capitulated, but the powerful Benchomo and the other menceyes of Tenerife were always on the watch for invaders, and the conquerors were forced to abandon their efforts to take over the island.

In 1494, when Fernández de Lugo arrived, the island was divided into nine menceydoms, or kingdoms: ANAGA, TEGUESTE, TACORONTE, TAORO, ICOD, DAUTE, ADEJE, ABONA and GUIMAR, each governed by a mencey, and an achimencey (Hidalgo, or knight) in Punta del Hidalgo.

The menceydoms of Anaga, Güímar, Abona and Adeje were «peaceful factions», since many years previously they had reached a pact and the process of of evangelization had begun. The menceydoms of Tegueste, Tacoronte and Taoro formed and alliance and Icod and Daute preferred to take care of their own defence.

Lugo's struggle was made easier thanks to the neutrality of the four menceydoms to whom he gave all the assurances he could. He had brought with him, 1.200 men, mostly Spaniards, with some islanders. He landed on the beaches of AÑAZO (Santa Cruz de Tenerife) where he encountered little resistance and decided to continue up to Aguere (La Laguna).

Benchomo appeared with three hundred men to see what Lugo wanted of him. Using Guillén Castellano as interpreter, Lugo assured him that he had come in friendship and entreated him and his people to become Christian and capitulate to the King of Spain. Benchomo replied that, «with regard to friendship, no man who was not provoked by another and angered had to flee nor decline this since it was to the common good; and that he would accept this in good will, if they were to leave his land, and leave him in peace and help themselves to what there was there, and he would be grateful. And with regard to being Christian, his people did not know what Christianity was, and did not understand this religion and thus with more understanding he would give a reply. But what they said about submitting to the King of Spain, they were not of this view, because never had they accepted submission to another man such as he»[41]. And so Benchomo left with his men.

Fernández de Lugo decided to advance into the valley ruled by Benchomo. He passed through Tegueste and Tacoronte without encountering resistance, and reached Orotava or Taoro, where everything was peaceful. Here they rounded up some livestock and decided to turn back.

Once they reached the gully of Acentejo, though, they were met by a force of three hundred Guanches sent ahead by Benchomo under the command of his brother CHIMENCIA[42] (TINGUARO). Without further ado, the Guanches launched into a violent attack, scattering the stolen livestock and not giving the Spaniards time to reach for their weapons. Benchomo arrived shortly with the rest of his men, throwing the opposing forces into confusion and killing some nine hundred Christians. The three hundred odd men who were left managed to escape, including about ninety Canarios.

Alonso de Lugo exchanged his clothes with a Canario and, although severely wounded in the mouth, made good his escape, whilst the Canario was pursued and finally killed. Together with some of his men, Lugo took refuge in the fort of Santa Cruz and later left to seek reinforcements.

The Guanches found thirty Spaniards hiding in a cave and Benchomo commanded them to be handed over at Añazo.

With so few people left to him, Lugo had no alternative but to withdraw.

THE RETURN OF LUGO AND
THE BATTLE OF LA LAGUNA

Fernández de Lugo returned with around seven hundred Spaniards and more islanders, a somewhat similar number of troops to those he had brought with him previously. As soon as he reached Añazo, he made up his mind to go up to La Laguna, where the Guanches, alerted to his arrival, were waiting.

The forces of Benchomo and his allies numbered more than five thousand men and during the ferocious battle that followed many Guanches were lost. The valiant Benchomo, that day, fought seven men and, badly wounded, fled to the slopes of San Roque where he was killed by Captain Buendía.

The Guanches withdrew, seeing that it was futile to continue the fight in such unfavourable terrain; also, brave CHIMENCIA had died in the battle. Subsequently they named BENTOR, son of Benchomo, mencey[43].

The Spaniards, cut the head from Benchomo's body and sent it to his kingdom as a means of persuading his people to capitulate, but their reply was that «where the body had remained so should remain the head; that they were not frightened by this; rather, that each one should look to his own»[44].

Alonso de Lugo withdrew to Santa Cruz with his men and stayed there for some months without attempting any new venture. His soldiers, greatly affected by the series of disasters, wanted to abandon the idea of the conquest.

THE SECOND BATTLE OF ACENTEJO

It has been said that the number of corpses left after the battle of La Laguna caused the outbreak of some epidemic in the area and that maybe it was for this reason that the Spaniards decided not to advance to the valley of Taoro. But in view of the grave setback they had suffered in Acentejo, they were doubtless reluctant to approach areas where the Guanches were strong and, moreover, waiting for them.

For a while they only made a few raids on the menceydoms of Tegueste and Tacoronte. Then, at last, Lugo decided to penetrate into the valley where the menceyes from the north were preparing for the great battle. The soldiers took leave of one another since it was Lugo's intention to win or to die in the attempt.

The site chosen was very close to that of the previous battle in Acentejo. Lugo divided his troops into two units, with himself in command of one and Lope Hernández de la Guerra in command of the other.

The battle commenced, with the Spaniards in a very strong position thanks to the use of fire-arms which they had primed earlier. After some hours of combat they realized that they were winning and started to shout «Victory!».

The Guanches who were not taken prisoner fled to the refuge of the mountains. There were many dead, according to ESPINOSA.

The battle took place on 25th December, 1495. So it was at this point that the luck of the Spaniards changed. Only a few pockets of resistance remained, with the majority of Guanche warriors staying in hiding in the mountains.

The mencey Bentor, who had taken refuge in the high regions of his kingdom, saw that hope was lost and in a ritual act of suicide hurled himself down into a ravine close to Tigaiga.

The conquest of the Canary Islands lasted, in all, ninety-four years, beginning in 1402 and ending in 1496. And the Spaniards themselves ended by admiring the men who had fought so fiercely in defence of the liberty of their homelands, some of whom had preferred to die rather than be taken into slavery. Men who were also remembered for their generosity and the mercy they had shown their enemies when taking them prisoner.

In a reference to the conquest, Espinosa said, «... the war that the Spaniards made... on the natives of these islands... was unjust, unreasonable... because these people neither owned Christian lands, nor passed over their limits and boundaries to invade or disturb others. So to say that they brought them the Gospel should have been by means of preaching... and not with the drum and the banner...»[45].

THIRD SECTION

COLONIZATION AND SURVIVAL OF THE GUANCHES

ANALYSIS OF THE CONQUEST

No exact information exists about the inhabitants of the Canary Islands. We only have a rough knowledge of the people of each island but not of all of them in general.

If the island of Lanzarote had some three hundred warriors at the time Bethencourt arrived, it is supposed that there were not many inhabitants there, perhaps not many more than a thousand. Fuerteventura had many more inhabitants than Lanzarote but neither do we have any real facts about this island. And no one knows how many people there were in El Hierro although it is believed that there were not many.

There were few deaths at the time of the conquest and the native peoples soon adapted to the new society.

As we have seen, La Gomera proved very difficult to subjugate and although there were indeed many deaths and captives taken, the people, in the main, continued to be mostly native.

Gran Canaria, La Palma and Tenerife, with greater populations than the other islands, also had many more problems.

At the time of the conquest, Gran Canaria must have had somewhere between twenty and thirty thousand inhabitants, that is, if we take into account the several thousand fighting men.

A fertile island such as La Palma could easily have had from six to eight thousand inhabitants or even more, since in some of the provinces there were a great many men.

Tenerife, of necessity, must have had around thirty thousand inhabitants, for if Benchomo alone could assemble some five thousand men, even though some of these would have belonged to the forces of Tegueste and Tacoronte, it must be supposed that there were several other thousands in the rest of the island, especially in Güímar. And knowing that there were so many warriors, it is unreasonable to assume that there was less than the above mentioned number living on the island.

The Archipielago would have had, in all, somewhere around seventy thousand inhabitants or maybe more.

An analysis would show that there was not an excessive number of deaths in combat except in certain battles.

If we are to refer to the chroniclers of the various battles in Gran

Canaria, according to Galindo, three hundred men died at Guiniguada and, according to Gómez Escudero, only thirty. In the battle in which Doramas died, there were not too many deaths but this would be due to the fact that he was killed early on in the combat.

And there were few deaths in other battles since the warriors surrendered to the man who had, after all, been their guanarteme.

In Tenerife, however, there were two battles which resulted in a considerable number of deaths: the battle of La Laguna, and the second battle, at Acentejo. It is possible, though, that the chroniclers tended to exaggerate the number of deaths, most likely in order to insinuate that more Guanches were killed at Acentejo than Spaniards.

In La Palma, few men died in combat because there were no great confrontations.

In any case, though, there were not so many deaths as have been imagined. Most of the warriors were taken captive, some fled to the mountains and other gave themselves up. There were some, who chose to die: they hurled themselves into space from the mountain-side or settled in caves to die of hunger, but they were in a minority.

THE SITUATION OF THE GUANCHES
AFTER THE CONQUEST

«From the time that Juan de Bethencourt initiated the conquest in 1402, the situation would vary in the face of the impossibility of reducing to slavery the entire population of the islands of Lanzarote and Fuerteventura... By about 1423 the greater part of the primitive population of Lanzarote, Fuerteventura and Hierro was convertd to Christianity»[46].

The situation of the islands' indigenous inhabitants depended as well on their conduct at the time of the conquest. «However, a substantial difference must be noted between the conquests of Gran Canaria, La Palma and Tenerife. In the former island, liberty depended on the personal attitude taken by the natives. The peaceful faction was respected, as were those who capitulated peacefully and under assurance. In La Palma and Tenerife, liberty depended on belonging to a delimited geographic area. The inhabitants of the territories declared «peaceful factions» would be free. All the other indigenous peoples were reduced to captivity as slaves of «fair war», independent of the attitude they had adopted at the moment of fighting and resistance»[47].

Lugo, however, respected neither the men who had assisted him nor those who had remained neutral, and ended up capturing more than a thousand men from the «peaceful factions». He kept some three hundred of these in Tenerife, and Juan de Guzmán, Duke of Medina Sidonia, secreted a considerable number of them on his property at Sanlúcar de Barrameda[48].

When the King and Queen of Castile were notified of this by Rodrigo de Betanzos, they ordered these Guanches, who were Christians, to be set free. The Guanches of Tenerife were swiftly released, but those on the mainland were freed later, after a long investigation[49].

The indigenous peoples did not adapt easily to urban life and there was a great feeling of solidarity amongst them. They were in the habit of stealing their overlords' livestock and giving it to the free Guanches. In the year 1500, the Cabildo (Council) of Tenerife stipulated that «... no male or female Guanche could be free without first giving sixteen years' service to their overlord,...»[50].

Punishment was most severe in certain cases. «... any slave who flees from today on shall die and the tribunal shall pay his master and if the slave is female she shall be given one hundred lashes and cast out from the land»[51]. In 1504 it was made public that all free Guanches «... be set to work for pay... and leave whence they were hidden and go outside the village with the charge that were they not to comply they would be captive for a certain time, the half of that money for the person returning them and the other half for themselves»[52]. Another measure decided by the Cabildo involved replacing Guanche herdsmen by Castilians, giving them four months's grace, «... because the Guanche herdsmen are thieves and rob all the island and destroy the livestock of which all the people complain, and until now it has not been made good by Castilian herdsmen for the lack of them»[53]; but this was not put into practice and everything continued as it was. Then, in 1507, the Cabildo decided to remove the act of prohibition by which the Guanche slaves were unable to travel around outside their masters' properties.

One of the first steps taken by the colonists was to move the local people around from one island to another, since keeping them away from the island of their birth they were more easily kept in order. Certain free, or banished, slaves were also transferred to other islands.

A fair-sized group of Canarios who had been brought over to Tenerife for the conquest tried to return to their island.

«These Canarios, dwelling in Tenerife, once the island had been pacified, constituted a respected and influential minority who always asserted their claim to treatment on a parity with the Castilians»[54].

Also living in Tenerife were groups of Gomeros and Palmeros, and in Gran Canaria there were Gomeros and a considerable number of Tinerfeños in Arguineguín[55]. The indigenous slaves in the islands were numerous but there were many of them, too, in Seville and other parts of Southern Spain who were ketp as exiles and slaves.

Pedro de Vera even banished women and children from Gran Canaria to Seville to have them converted to Christianity and get rid of them, but in 1485 Fernando Guanarteme pleaded in Court on behalf of his former vassals and the King and Queen of Castile took steps «to remedy this and also so that they do not continue assembling performing actions and communities of heathendom that they are in the habit of, Juan Guillén, mayor of Seville, is assigned the task of dealing exclusively with the said Canarios, protecting them from all danger, seeking masters for them, each one with his master and husband and wife together; and with the unmarried men, separating them from the women that they do not marry «en facie ecclesia»; and punishing judiciously those who act badly while they do not know Christian doctrine and customs»[56].

Other Guanches remained on their islands. It is to be supposed that the few colonists there were, were unable to control too closely the great number of native peoples.

«Bishop Juan de Frías and Governor Pedro de Vera divided the male and female Canary children between the islands' residents to persuade them to the faith and instruct them in the Christian doctrine, giving the married men with their wives the female Canary children and the unmarried men the male Canary children, in order to indoctrinate them»[57].

In conclusion, despite the outrages and acts of injustice committed by the colonists, there were thousands of native people, both slaves and free, who contributed to the formation of a new social and economic structure.

COLONIZATION AND DIVISION OF LANDS

As we have already seen, the people of the first islands conquered by Juan de Bethencourt were in a different situation from those in La Palma, Tenerife and Gran Canaria.

We only have the evidence of the conquerors and colonists themselves, plus that some of native islanders who were lucky when it came to handing out land and water rights. Unfortunately, little is known about all the slaves kept on the colonists' extensive properties, and this has led to a general belief that the majority of the primitive peoples disappeared, leaving only the colonists and a few remaining natives in the Canary Islands.

The colonists in any case, did not attach too much importance to the indigenous peoples who were, as far as they were concerned, nothing more than heathens and, with a few exceptions, not sufficiently human to be worthy of consideration.

There were not so many colonists as has been generally supposed.

When Gran Canaria was conquered, six hundred men arrived on the island. Two hundred men from Biscay were the next to arrive, followed by some two hundred reinforcements[59].

A great number of these men were to die in the islands, most of them in the fort of AJODAR[59] where the majority of the men from Biscay perished. If we calculate that there were a thousand men in all, only just over seven hundred survived and of these, Vera sent most of them back to Spain[60].

In later years a few other colonists settled on the islands to exploit the natural wealth.

In the earliest partitions, great chunks of land and extensive water rights were granted to some thirty people, including, according to information we have about Gran Canaria, the governor Pedro de Vera[61]. Many partitions were made subsequently but it is nevertheless accepted that the number of colonists was vastly inferior to the native population, both free and slaves.

Events in Tenerife and Gran Canaria were somewhat similar. Fernández de Lugo brought seven hundred men over from Spain, with a few colonists from the other islands which had been conquered, plus another seven hundred other islanders, at least. This time, most of the conquerors stayed alive but there were nonetheless several who left. «But now that the island was calm, most of the soldiers returned to Castile, to their homes, and those who wished to stay were granted residence and partition of lands»[62]. The land was equally divided between settlers and families from other islands as well as amongst natives who had come over for the conquest. These few hundred colonists were the same as those of La Palma and, as a consequence, most of the best land remained in their hands.

From the «DATAS» (partitions) of Tenerife it can be ascertained that there were not too many colonists. Distribution of lands began in 1497 and after nearly twenty years still had not reached, 1.900 partitions, including those of La Palma. Certain colonists, too, received a fair number of different partitions in various places. In the 1.900 odd partitions must be included, as we have said, lands given to many of the natives who had taken part in the conquest as well as to others in Tenerife who were given property after a period of service to their masters.

If most of the conquerors were returned to the mainland both from Gran Canaria and from Tenerife, this would mean that some three hundred were left on each island. And if the majority of these colonists who remained were to have married native women, as it is said, then we are only dealing with a small élite of colonists who later brought over their families, masons, carpenters etc. and some Portuguese to manage their large properties and sugar cane refineries. If we take into consideration that each colonist had several slaves working for him as labourers, then this must mean that the number of colonists was considerably lower than the number of natives. Neither should we forget the indigenous peoples belonging to the various «peaceful factions», who were in any case free and, of course, all those who remained in hiding, who belonged to the «warring factions».

DETAILS OF SOME OF THE PARTITIONS MADE
NATIVES OF THE ISLANDS (GUANCHES)

Item N°. 1.326: Elvira Hernández, sister of Pedro el Bueno, and of Gaspar Hernández, my servants, natives of this island; you are my goddaughter and wish to marry and for the good service you have done me I give you 400 fanegas (Trans. note: 1 fanega equals 1.59 acres) of land in Abona...

Item N°. 576: Diego de Bauten, native of this island... 60 fanegas of land for sowing...

Item N°. 306: María de Lugo, wife of Pedro, deceased, natives of the island of Tenerife, 100 fanegas of unirrigated land in the district of Adexe...

Item N°. 1.303: Pedro Martín, native of this island, and Francisco Delgado, my servant, I give some caves...

Item N°. 40: Miguel of Agoymad (Güímar) resident and native of this island, two «cahices» (Trans. note: a very small piece of land) of unirrigated land.

Item N°. 720: Pedro Abtejo, Gomero, resident of this island of Tenerife, abode of 8 fanegas of unirrigated land...

Item N°. 1.292: Francisco Hara, Gomero, 1 give 4 cahices of unirrigated land which are in three... I state that I give you 30 fanegas...

Item N°. 151: Fernando, slave. I, the governor, give thanks to you, Fernando, my slave, with one fanega of irrigated land next to your cave...

Item N°. 362: Alonso de Córdoba, Canario from Gran Canaria, one cahice in Taoro...

Item N°. 694: Martín Cosmes and Diego Delgado, Canarios, my servants. A piece of land...

Item N°. 906: Antonio Díaz, Canario and conqueror. A slope of lands in Acentejo.

Item N°. 272: Juan Uramas (Doramas), Rodrigo the Lame, Francisco de León and Fernando de León... Canarios... we entreat you to favour us with some lands...

Item N°. 664: Juan Fernández, Canario...

Item N°. 669: Guillén García, Canario...

Item N°. 813: Alonso González, Canario...

Item N°. 868: Pedro de Lugo, Canario...

Item N°. 454: Diego de Manzanilla, Pedro de Manenidra, «I, the governor, Alonso de Lugo... give you...»

Item N°. 913: Pablo Martín, Canario...

Item N°. 824: Martín Cosmes, Juan Ramos, Diego Pestano, Martín de Vera y Rodríguez García, Canarios...

Item N°. 1.845: Gonzalo de la Fuente, and Juan Sánchez, Canarios (15-1-1506)...

Item N°. 69: Pedro Camacho... native of Gran Canaria...

Item N°. 17: Fernando Guanarteme... give you... 60 fanegas of land for sowing on the slopes of Acentejo...

Item N°. 845: Diego of Adexe... we give and promise to you, don Diego,... who was king of Adexe in the island of Tenerife,... 30 fanegas of land with water...[63]

Partition of lands was made to a few other Tinerfeños and many more natives of Gran Canaria.

In conclusion, it would seem that only a few thousand colonists must have settled on the islands with a cheap labour force made up of slaves to plough the land and care for the livestock.

MEASURES TAKEN BY THE CROWN IN FAVOUR OF THE INDIGENOUS PEOPLES

Right from the beginning the Church played a most important rôle in protecting the indigenous peoples of the Canary Islands from the ill-treatment of the colonists.

In 1477, Fernán Peraza captured some hundred Gomeros, both men and women, and shipped them to Seville; Bishop Juan Frías got to know about it however and presented himself at the Spanish Court to plead that they be set free. He was successful and the Gomeros were handed over to him in person, and he ordered that those who had been already sold should be handed over, too, and the money paid for them returned[64].

Isabel la Católica (Queen of Castile) declared: «It has been related to us and we are informed that some persons have been brought... Canarios... who are Christians and others who are on their way to converting to our Holy Catholic Faith... and they sell them as slaves... and as such a thing would set a bad example and would serve to deter people from wanting to convert to the Holy Catholic Faith, we are desirous of remedying this... and we agree to command this our decree... Therefore we order that every and any person... who... is brought... you shall not consent them being sold...»[65].

The Gomeros were returned to the Islands in June, 1478, but Pedro de Vera retained them in Las Palmas until the Catholic King and Queen commanded him to take them back to La Gomera[66].

The accusations against Pedro de Vera, which were certainly made by Bishop Frías led to the establishment of an investigating commission which, with the assistance of Spanish noblemen and attorneys acting in defence of the indigenous peoples, reached a decision favourable to the Canarios[67].

Fernán Peraza, lord of La Gomera, had carried out many acts of outrage against the natives of this island and, weary of the continual maltreatment, they made up their minds to kill him. They learned that he enjoyed a relationship with Princess Yballa and in 1488, when once he visited her cave, they slew him.

The wife of Peraza, Beatriz de Bobadilla, requested the help of Pedro de Vera in punishing the men who had killed her husband. They killed some and captured about four hundred others showing no respect for those who were not guilty and sold them as slaves. These, too, were able to recover their freedom after a long investigation ordered by the King and Queen, with the assistance of attorneys, bishops and missionaries[68].

As a result of the many outrages, the King and Queen ordered the lady Bobadilla to pay 500.000 maravedíes (Trans. note: old Spanish coinage) by way of compenstion to the Gomeros.

Another consequence was the removal of one of the conquerors, Pedro de Vera, governor of Gran Canaria.

Some information about two of the menceyes has been recorded: Diego de Adeje (Diego of Adeje) and Fernando de Anaga (Fernando of Anaga). The latter was forced to take up residence in Gran Canaria and «Lugo captured his son, Enrique de Anaga. He was freed in 1501, thanks to the impassioned intervention of Bachelor Alonso de Sepúlveda, Attorney at Court for the poor, whom the Hispanic Monarchs had specially commissioned to liberate Palmenses and Guanches from the clutches of the oppressors»[69].

«These outrages and this commission had their echo in the 'trial of residence' undergone by the governor of Tenerife and governor-general of the Canaries, Alonso Fernández de Lugo, in 1508, by royal command. The governor of Gran Canaria and special judge, López de Sosa, sentenced him to making a payment of 40.000 maravedíes to the 'sons of the king of Adeje'. Another native of royal line, Andrés de Güímar, in the same verdict was awarded 50.000 maravedíes as compensation»[70].

Lugo was also responsible for ill-treating a prince of La Palma, Pedro Fernández de La Palma, son of one of the island's chiefs, but the notice was brought to Court by Gazmira, who was living in Madrid. «And at the time that Alonso de Lugo... set off to conquer the said island, the said Canarios of the said factions united with him and helped him to make the conquest until such a point that the said island was subdued and conquered; and that thus... the Canarios of one of the said factions became Christians and the men married their women in accordance with the order of the Holy Church and still many of the said Canarios of the other faction as well became Christians»[71].

Lugo captured another two hundred natives from the «peaceful factions» by inventing false pretexts, but Gazmira was able to make his voice heard at Court[72].

With the intervention of Rodrigo de Betanzos, who brought the news to Court and took on the responsibility of defending the indigenous peoples, the three hundred natives in Lugo's possession were swiftly freed[73].

In the year 1500, Licentiate Maluenda and Bachelor Sepúlveda continued to act in defence of the freedom of the Palmenses and Guanches at the court of Seville. When the investigations began there, the various masters transferred their slaves elsewhere, however later the informants were able to obtain authority to seek them out wherever they were, outside Seville.

Pedro Fernández de La Palma, whom we have already mentioned, together with two other natives, Miguel Martín and Leonor Morales, in 1502 started to make their voices heard in support of the oppressed Palmenses and Guanches[74].

After the long fight maintained by the natives and their tireless defenders, Rumeu de Armas said of the verdict:

«There is more than enough evidence, however, to believe and estimate that all was in favour of the natives. In the first place this is based on belief in the spirit of justice which was so beloved of the people in all the kingdom and a veritable obsession with its eminent leaders. In the second place, on the precedent set by Gomeros and Gran Canarios, for whose liberty they fought and won in court, at the Royal Counsel, and at other tribunals. Why would the Palmenses and Guanches, in invoking such just motives, receive different treatment? The third reason is a weighty argument: the protests were suddenly eclipsed and not one voice was heard which begged for liberty and justice on behalf of the victims. This in itself is equivalent to a 'sentence'»[75].

THE GUANCHES IN HIDING

Upon realizing that no hope was left of throwing the invaders off the island, large numbers of the Guanches belonging to the «warring factions» went into hiding in the mountains, and despite the efforts of Lugo to capture them, he was, with a few, rare exceptions unsuccessful, although certain nambers of them did turn themselves in from time to time.

In 1499, «The situation was extremely serious in view of the large number of natives in hiding who had fled to the mountains and were living in freedom, taking adventage of their proverbial and better knowledge of the terrain»[76]. In the same year, «Lugo ordered by decree a further conquest, respecting the 'peaceful factions'... the lieutenant of the governor, Gerónimo Valdés, proposed using various Guanches in whom he could trust as auxiliary guides; but he met with the protest of the jury, Juan de Badajoz, who saw in the measure more danger than profit»[77].

This scheme did not result in anything and was never carried out. The magistrate even said that he would expel the supposed collaborators from the island, and Lugo's plans were thus blocked[78]. This is corroborated by N° 494 of the Cabildo records entered in 1506, which states that «... there are many Guanches hiding in the island who rob livestock and do other damage...»[79].

In the words of Rumeu de Armas, «... there was no real solution to the problem of the Guanches in hiding because they came under the protection of the peaceful natives at the first trace of danger. The agreements of the Cabildo alluded to them over many years with wearisome insistence. Their incorporation into the nascent society as free men was to be a thing of time and still not to take place for several decades»[80].

In the island of La Palma, the hidden aborigines in the mountains, and specially the people of chief Tanausu from Taburiente Crater, were able to survive the cold weather because there are big caves between the «Cumbrecita» and «Pico de la Nieve» which keep a certain natural warmth during the winter.

According to the oral transmision that has reached the present day through shepherds (generation after generation), the cave «El Jumo» is bare all around and was the native people's refuge when the Spanish set fire to the mountain so that they would give up.

THE RETURN OF THE NATIVE PEOPLES TO THE CANARY ISLANDS

The natives who were slaves in the mainland or had been banished there were constantly fighting to be given their freedom and the right to return to their place of birth.

As it has been said, Pedro de Vera banished quite a number of natives from Gran Canaria to Seville including women and children. These people started returning to the island but Pedro de Vera, fearing conflict, managed to put a halt to their arrival, contending that they were fewer in number than the natives living on the island and could rise in revolt against him. against him.

Several hundred Canarios who had been banished from the islands returned but were compelled to take part in the conquest of La Palma and Tenerife[81].

The natives insisted so strongly on returning that it can be supposed that as soon as their claims for freedom had been settled, they would have tried to reach the islands. This would have been a slow process, though.

Speaking about the slaves, Manuela Marrero said, «... the slave endeavours and secures his liberty often by his own means»[82].

They also paid to obtain their freedom and then, too, many families who were in liberty did their utmost to ensure their relations were set free, and sometimes would set off for the mainland to find them[83].

We can see from the following how many slaves from the «peaceful factions» were sought by their families. «Diego Díaz, Fernán Pérez, Miguel de Guímar, Alonso de Bonilla, Fernando de Ibaute, Juan Alonso, Bastián de Ortega, Pedro de Trujillo, Juan de las Casas, Pedro de Llarena, Fernán de Tegueste, Alonso González, Francisco de Adexe, Diego de Armas, Juan Osorio,... give special authority to Andrés de Güimar... that he appear before the Queen and her Counsel and make all the necessary enquiries in the action for the liberty of the peaceful Guanches which has been followed against the governor»[84].

Many of the Guanches who came back from banishment or slavery returned to wearing their former style of dress (the tamarco), they mingled with those in hiding in the mountains and advised the slaves to hide amongst them and steal their masters' livestock, since this was what the latter had stolen from them in the first place.

As can be proved in the documents of the island of La Palma's Town Council, the Alderman Luis Alvarez presented a royal schedule received on the 2nd. of november 1577 in which the Royal Highness had given permision to carry through a sale of 500 slaves, for a limited period, for 13.000 «ducados» (currency at the time), to build a port in the capital of this island. (Council records dated December the 4th 1579). This petition had been made by the previous Alderman, Luis Horosco, who had made an application to the Royal Highness to build the mentioned port.

In the year 1587, Fernán Rodríguez, neighbour of Seville who had been commissioned for this matter, gave the island of La Palma's Council the money obtained from the sale of the forementioned slaves.

If nearly a century after the Spanish colonisation, they could sell this number of slaves, taking into account the few thousand inhabitants this island had, it is clearly demonstrated that the number of indegenous were superior to the foreigners. These slaves, as can be seen, were sold for a limited period and would soon return.

Many of those Portuguese and Spaniards who were arriving at the Canary Islands, after the conquest, apparently as colonisers, were real guanches who after having learnt different trades during their barnishment or slavery time returned after many years making use of certain privileges. This has also been confirmed by the historian Lothar Siemens Hernández who refering to XV century documents found in the Island of Madeira assures that many years before the Canary Island conquest, Portuguese people captured a few hundred natives to populate the Island of Madeira and employed them as shepherds. These slaves returned to the Canary Islands, or their decendants, as skilled workers in the cane-sugar industry and with Portuguese surnames.

THE ADAPTATION TO THE NEW SOCIETY AND UNITING OF THE NATIVES AND THE COLONISTS

As soon as the conquest was over, the natives had to face a new and substantial change in their lives. At the beginning, apart from a small, indigenous minority that had mixed with or accommodated itself to the new society, it was more difficult for some of the natives to adapt than it was for others. Very few years after the conquest, many natives were being integrated into the new society. «The free natives not only devoted themselves to herding and selling their products to the residents who had arrived on the island, but the latter also, gradually, expanded their agricultural labours in order to attain the higher standard of living enjoyed by the foreigner.

«They have bought lands with the return from the raising of livestock or by donation or partition as resident»[85].

the customs of and progress made by the conquerors, and began to take part in urban life, the learned ones amongst them taking up duties whilst serving their overlords as slaves or servants; apart from those in hiding, however, there were the free herdsmen who kept up their old way of life in the high, isolated, regions. In 1514, the Cabildo still forbade the natives from the mountains to carry arms because they had no dealings with the Spaniards; they followed old traditions and still wore their TAMARCOS[86].

From the very outset of the new society, many colonists married native women, although not so many as had been hoped. Even if we consider that most of the colonists were bachelors and that they were the ones who married here, we must remember that there were some seven hundred men in Gran Canaria and as many again in La Palma and Tenerife, most of whom returned to the mainland a few months after the conquest was over. Therefore it would appear that on these three islands not more than a few hundred marriages, or mixed marriages, took place. The marriages took place mostly between natives who had been integrated into the new society, either as slaves or as free men, but of course the people who lived in the mountains continued to marry amongst themselves.

Another point worth mentioning is that right at the beginning the islands' nobles had married Castilians.

In Gran Canaria, the daughter of Fernando Guanarteme, Guayarmina, baptized Margarita, married Miguel de Trexo Carvajal.

The native Arminda (Catalina) married Hernando de Guzmán, son of an eminent Castilian.

The daughter of the «guaire», Utindana, baptized Catalina Fernández, married Captain Francisco de Cabrejas.

In Lanzarote, descendants of the king, Guadarfía, united with the new overlords and leaders of the islands.

In Tenerife, one daughter of Bencomo (Benchomo), by the name of Dácil, married Gaspar Hernández, formerly king of Abona, and the other, María, married Juan Doramas, son of the valiant Doramas of Gran Canaria.

Pedro Maninidra, the famous warrior of Gran Canaria, had two children, Pedro and Inés.

Inés married Miguel González, a native of Gran Canaria, and of this union was born Agustín Delgado, famous conqueror of America.

Amongst other famous islanders were Ibone de Armas, son of Juan Negrín, a native of La Gomera[87].

To these marriages and adaptations to the new society is unfortunately linked the «Inquisition».

«It is a sad fact that in the proofs of nobility required to enter the colleges, it was necessary to vouch that one was not descended from Canary, Moorish nor Jewish blood, and this stipulation must have powerfully influenced the island populations to conceal their true affiliation, with the exception of those families cited above and others whom we may remenber were the descendants of guanartemes and menceyes, who of course had been ennobled and already occupied an exceptional position by reason of their alliances.

«The Inquisition for its part also contributed to this sad outcome, since it hastened to enter on its secret registers the converted Canarios, regarding them with a suspicious lack of confidence. The fear of appearing on these odious lists and suffering the bitter deceptions which were their inevitable consequence, contributed pitifully to the concealment of «noted» surnames, to the supplanting of parents and grandparents and to the invention of genealogical trees so fantastic as to be ridiculous»[88].

More than pitiful, this is shameful; the Guanches in no way deserved such unjust discrimination, for both free men and those who had been slaves for many years, found themselves denied the same rights as Castilians and were consequently reduced to second-class status.

It can also be seen how some Canarios disclaimed their own race and even went so far as to change the surnames which distinguished them. This was doubtlessly the motive that led the Canarios, or at least a majority of them, within only a few decades claiming' to be true Castilians and indisposed to admit their Guanche origin. This discriminatory policy enormously favoured the overlords, the conquerors, since one of their first propositions was to put an end to the primitive complex. And thus the islanders were quickly assimilated into Spanish culture, whether voluntarily or under obligation.

It is easy, therefore, to infer the motives which caused the concept of the Guanches as we now know them to disappear. Furthermore, the natives who took to Spanish dress and followed Spanish customs were no longer considered to be Guanches. And we should bear in mind that the natives or rather, their children, certainly would have been taunted and ridiculed for some of their ancestral traditions.

Brother Alonso de Espinosa said of Guanche customs, «This is what, of the customs of the natives, with much difficulty and work, I have been able to learn and comprehend because the old Guanches are so shy and intimidated that if they do know them they do not wish to say, thinking that to divulge them is detrimental to their nation»[89].

THE CANARY POPULATION IN THE FIRST DECADES OF THE 16TH CENTURY

I have been unable to ascertain how many inhabitants there were shortly after the conquest.

In this third volume of history. Agustín Millares Torres speacks of the year 1522: «I5t is reasonable to infer, as hypothesis, that in those years there lived some twenty-five thousand inhabitants on the islands of the archielago...»[90].

This is, then, an hypothetical figure although, in fact, the number of inhabitants cannot have been much greater. They had no census in those days and we can only refer to the registers.

First of all, we must remember that in 1522 there could have been a fairly high number of natives living in hiding, then we must consider the decades it took these people to integrate into the new society as free men. And the colonists certainly would not have taken too much trouble to find out how many free Guanches were living in for-off areas.

Owing to the colonization of America, the Canary Islands underwent certain changes. Firstly, the colonization by Castilians was, to a great extent, halted, and the Portuguese arrived instead, as we have mentioned. This was because the Spaniards did not want to waste any opportunity to chance the fortune in the fertile lands of America and, with the wealth of the Canaries already han led out and exploited by the colonists, it was unlikely that their children would enjoy the same well-being. Emigration to the new continent was plentiful, a great many of the pioneers being the children of colonists and the Guanches who had been integrated into the new society.

Then, on the islands, we have the natives who still lived in hiding and those who returned from the mainland. These isolated herdsmen were not amongst the first to emigrate to America; they preferred the peaceful lives they were leading.

In this way, the Canary population remained fairly stable throughout those years and continued to be so for a good while longer for it was said than in 1540 there were some 40.000 inhabitants in the archipielago.

THE CANARY PEOPLE AT THE END OF THE LAST CENTURY

The Guanches, as we have mentioned, were gradually integrated into the new society but for certain groups of them this took many years.

Nearly a century after the conquest of Tenerife, there was a group in Candelaria that continued to follow the old customs. Father Espinosa met them and speaks of the island's villages: «Candelaria and Güímar are on the other side, places where the remaining native Guanches are living, who are few in number because they are already mixed...»[91].

Numerous traditions have survived to the present day or, rather, until a few decades ago.

At the end of the last century there were still Canary people who followed many of the old customs.

In Gran Canaria, between 1885 and 1888, Victor Grau Bassas lived with the people in the countryside and wrote a book about his experiences.

He said of their dwellings, «In Gran Canaria there are two types of abodes: some in caves, others in houses built of stone and clay. The caves are rooms built into the rock, using those made by the old inhabitants and building some new ones...»[92].

About their form of dress he tells us, «The headgear is the most useless and irksome piece of the old clothing that is known; calling attention as it has lasted until today»[93]. (The author was comparing it with the leather cap used by the Guanches).

«The shirt is an ordinary man's shirt made of linen material woven in the country. These shirts have very long tails and one can wear just this without being offensive for they reach mid-calf»[94]. (The shape was similar to that of the former garment but the material used was different).

«Few peoples exist in the world more restrained than the Canary people. In this they have followed point by point the old traditions, and in them they greatly resemble their relatives, the present Bedouins[95].

«In every kind of meal the indispensable and most essential part is the gofio, and this is kneaded with milk or whey, with potatoes, with soup etc.

«The table is prepared on the ground on a palm mat, which is never missing even in the most miserable of caves. This is covered by a white cloth around in which sits the whole family: the women with their legs crossed and the men stretched out and leaning on their left elbow»[96].

Doctor R. Vernau was also in the Canaries in the last century and visited all the islands to which he refers, where he found everywhere the Guanche physiognomy.

In Fuerteventura, as in earlier times, the people were the tallest in the islands. «The people of Fuerteventura resemble those of Lanzarote in their customs and dress, but they differ physically. It is not unusual to find on this island men of great height who often exceed 1.75 metres and who, in their physiognomy and the characteristics of their skulls, remind us singularly of the ancient Guanches»[97].

In his visit to Tenerife, he tells us: «... we arrived at a poor cabin of dried stone where we were received with the utmost cordiality. We were in the village of Anaga... Our host was a herdsman and one of the poorest of this spot lost amid the mountains, but he had the worth and the generosity of his Guanche antecedents... one did not need a strong imagination to believe oneself in the house of a descendant of the worthy herdsmen of earlier times. If he did not wear the garment, he was certainly of the type...»[98].

Herdsman from Mogán (Gran Canaria).

Man from the island of El Hierro, in summer clothing.

R. Verneau, pp. 173 and 273, «Cinco años de estancia en las Islas Canarias». Ediciones J.A.D.L.; La Orotava, Tenerife.

50

In reference to the fair people of the North of Tenerife and, more specifically, in San Juan de la Rambla, he says, «What most startled me, when I arrived for the first time, was the fairly considerable number of individuals with blue eyes and fair hair. Their height, their features, all denotes that we were not in the presence of descendants of the conquerors[99].

«In Fasnia... the dwellings were excavated in the volcanic rock and the inhabitansts live in these caves in the same way as did the ancient Guanches... The people are hospitable, descended in part from the former islanders, whose type is preserved.

In the mid-sixteenth century, the Spaniards had ventured almost no further than Güímar. This locality, too, was inhabited by authentic Guanches who themselves formed a village»[100].

In Tenerife, «the inhabitants greatly resemble in all ways their neighbours in Gran Canaria. However, the Guanche type is observed with more frequency... one sees men so miserable... that they possess no other household goods than those of the ancient Guanches...»[101].

In Gran Canaria, he tells us of Mogán: «They are, above all, herdsmen in this place, where very few Europeans have settled. It is not unsusual to meet individuals who present, very markedly, the type of the former inhabitants, whose customs, too, they have preserved.

«The herdsman of Mogán can be considered the prototype of the Canary herdsman. He dresses in a shirt of heavy material, with breeches of the same material, of which each legging, as long as an underskirt, does not come below the knees, and a vest without sleeves[102].

«The inhabitants of La Gomera are very curious people. They remind one of their antecedents from before the conquest in their physical type and an infinity of customs. Short of stature, but agile and vigorous, they run with dizzying speed up and down the steepest ravines. In the characteristics of their heads, they resemble the Guanches...»[103].

SURVIVAL OF THE GUANCHE IN PRESENT TIMES

As can be seen from the previous chapter, towards the end of the last century there were still some herdsmen, especially in Gran Canaria, who wore garments similar to those of their Guanche ancestors.

Diego Cuscoy, in his book «Los Guanches», published in 1968, gives us an idea of the continuity of herding traditions up till the present day: «A people such as the Guanches given over entirely to pastoral activity, of necessity must have left traces of this[104].

«The pastoral way of life underwent upheaval as a result of the changes produced on the island by conquest and immediate colonization but it was maintained because it was an irreplaceable detail of the occupation and the livelihood of a great part of the island population... all of which meant that herding activities remained in the hands of the Guanches[105].

«This activity was practised especially in the «areas of Tacoronte, Tegueste, and Valle Guerra in the North and in the Valley of Arona and the Valley of Güímar in the South. Of more importance were the pastoral regions of the high mountains, above all Cañadas and the heights of La Guancha, Icod and Santiago del Teide... were open spaces, whose boundaries the native peoples had tried to preserve since the time of the Spanish conquest... thanks to the uninterrupted pastoral activity which has lasted until the present day»[106].

In recent times, several historians have vindicated the survival of the Guanches, thanks to numerous documents which have been found in official archives. The strictest silence has always surrounded the Guanche population or rather, shall we say, that what was known could not be published because it was not considered suitable for the general public to know the truth. Until only a very few years ago, the various publications on Canary history which reached the Canary people were lacking in adequate information. Even today, certain historians, quite incomprehensibly, speak of the «Guanche minorities» who survived, unfortunately basing their knowledge on the absurd and obstructive record of the Cabildo of Tenerife in 1515, in which it states that only six hundred Guanches remained on the island, including those in hiding, when in reality there is more than enough evidence to prove that this record is quite without foundation.

In his book on Canary history, Agustín Millares Torres tells us that a considerable number of natives survived in Fuerteventura and that in «La Gomera, controlled but not repopulated by foreign elements, the population continued in its great majority to be of indigenous origin, despite the rebellions, bondage and deportations...»[107]. Referring to the other islands, in particular, Gran Canaria and Tenerife, he says that apart from the groups that capitulated, the population made up of the «peaceful factions» continued to live in freedom as well as another group in Tacoronte, besides the herdsmen who remained in the isolated areas[108].

The distinguished professor, Rumeu de Armas, has stated publicly that ninety per cent. of the Canary population has Guanche blood and in a reference to Lugo's behaviour he says that «despite the overwhelming sympathy that the strong personality of the conqueror of Tenerife awakes, the most recent writing of history passes severe judgement on his conduct in relation to the indigenous peoples: a romantic attitude wishes to pass over these deeds in honour of the great historical significance of his name. But it is not possible that the present population of Tenerife, for the most part racially mixed, are the descendants of those who were his victims»[109].

The history of the Canary Islands in the early years after the conquest and, in particular, that of Gran Canaria, La Palma and Tenerife, was manipulated by the conquerors and their descendants over a long period.

They restricted themselves to references made to major events, although incorrectly. It is difficult to realize that there was not one single missionary or historian who was interested enough to relate everything which occurred. But then, if as we have seen, the Inquisition treated the Guanches as outcasts and they were thus compelled to deny their racial background, one can only suppose that it was equally forbidden to write about the savage treatment meted out by the colonists. The first historian to write about Tenerife was Brother Alonso de Espinosa, about a century after the conquest and, immediately afterwards, Torriani, Abreu Galindo etc.

If we draw up a brief analysis of all the facts collected in this book, we shall be able to see things more clearly:

First of all, if we speak of the Canary population, by comparing them before the conquest with the few decades following it, we can see that approximately two-thirds of the indigenous people disappeared. The colonists nonetheless still constituted a minority in the islands, as evinced by the partition of lands.

The two-thirds of the people on the islands who disappeared did not all perish, as we have seen, but were sold as slaves or banished to the mainland. If we work on the assumption that there were originally 70.000 inhabitants in the whole archipelago and take into account that there were not so many thousands of deaths, we can assume that many more people were sold into slavery than died.

And, as well, we have the protection afforded to the natives by the Crown. Ample evidence of this is the removal of the governor of Gran Canaria, Pedro de Vera, the compensation which the lady Bobadilla was ordered to pay and the trial of residence against Alonso Fernández de Lugo.

With the exclusion of the Guanches who remained free, the majority of the men were made slaves, although the colonists did not wish to dispense with them since they needed them badly to work the land and tend the livestock.

In the book Slavery in Tenerife, written by Manuela Marrero, it can be seen that the number of Guanche slaves diminished considerably from the year 1505 on. Between then and 1510 some fifty Guanches were sold into slavery and from 1510 to 1520, only about a dozen. The slaves used from then on, according to documents found, were Moorish, Berber, black and so on.

This makes one think that the large number of Guanches in hiding, who took such a long time to be incorporated into the new society, were fortunate enough to stay on their island if they were captured, or sold to colonists on other islands.

And then we have those Guanche slaves who fought so hard to be able to return to their islands. Many remained on the mainland, perhaps, but others preferred to return. We have already seen that the women and children of Gran Canaria came back to their island as soon as they were allowed to.

Lastly, a special mention must be made of the Guanche women and children. Could the Spaniards have been so fierce as to cause the disappearance of all those small children who were orphaned or, at least, without a father? No, not at all. Abreu Galindo has recounted how in Gran Canaria the children were shared out amongst the colonists. And we have, too, many accounts of the Spaniards' fair treatment of the Guanches who assisted them. So what makes us think that the slaves' children were not taken in by the colonists to be brought up and later turned into servants?

If we consider the hypothesis whereby Guanche women may have had problems in having children, owing to the tremendous changes they had to cope with, it must be stated that what happened in America did not happen in the Canaries; a proof of this is the number of marriages that took place between conquerors and Guanche women. And if these changes exerted some sort of influence on events, were not the Castilian women equally influenced by the idea of coming to live on islands in which the early years must of necessity have been somewhat disquieting?

The Gomeros, who proved so rebellious when the colonists tried to impose a different way of life on them and slew Peraza, their overlord, still survived, notwithstanding the deaths and maltreatment meted out to them. And, remembering that today the great majority of Gomeros are descended from the primitive peoples of the island, there is no cause to imagine that the other islands suffered worse treatment; references to the island indicate that La Gomera was one the most heavily sacked islands. Also, Lugo was able to intervene indirectly when he married Beatriz de Bobadilla, lady of La Gomera, after her husband's death, all the more so since he knew she would do all she could to avenge the assassination of Peraza.

As it happened, the colonists, although a minority, were the ones who were in control and compelled the islanders to drop their old customs. They forbade them to speak the old language or wear the leather garments they were used to. They forced them to live in villages that were not isolated from the rest of the community; they even obliged them to make Andalusian-style pottery. But despite all this, the Guanches were able to preserve. many traditions which have survived to the present day or, more specifically, until just a few decades ago.

Throughout the Canary Islands things have been preserved such as gofio, the stomach-bags of kids to knead it in, the stone mill to grind it in and certain words like: belete or tafor, the first milk goats produce; baifo, kid; gánigo, clay vessel; goro, yard, and others. The herdsmen have been the ones who have guarded the old customs most strictly: the long poles, the way of tending the goats and coating their teats with «tabaiba» milk (Trans. note: the tabaiba is an indigenous plant); this takes on a rubbery consistency and stops the kids from suckling in the daytime. The cloak used in La Esperanza is similar to the tamarco but today is not made of skins. Songs and dances also reflect considerable Guanche influence, most especially the «sirinoque», the «dance of the drum», the «vivo», the

54

«tajaraste» and even the «folía». The way Canary people speak today is reminiscent of the soft speech of the Guanches. The stick game is still played in much the same way as in former times. Canary wrestling also has pre-Hispanic roots, although it has evolved considerably since the conquest. And the generosity, hospitality and passivity of the Canary people are traits inherited from the primitive peoples in the islands.

So, from all this, we can deduce that despite so many deaths, and the slavery and upheavals suffered by the Guanche population during the period of transformation, the race lives on.

The physical features of the pre-Hispanic people are specially to be seen in poor regions and villages high up in the mountains where the people are of much purer stock. In Gran Canaria and Tenerife they tend to be found in the south of the island and in high regions. the so-called «tumulus culture» is also to be found on the North-West coast of Gran Canaria. These were people with very dark hair, broad noses and thick lips which «... displays a more 'African' stamp but with absolutely no negroid characteristics»[110]. Other places where the Guanche type can most be seen are La Vegueta, Haría, San Bartolomé, Tinajo and Teguise in Lanzarote; Tijarafe, Puntagorda and Garafía in La Palma; and all over the high regions of La Gomera. There are also plenty of pre-Hispanic types to be found in every village but these are not generally so pure. According to Dr. Schwidetzky, the people living in the surrounding districts of the islands' capitals have for the most part come from the country and pre-Hispanic physical traits are clear to be seen.

Strangers to the Canary Islands find no difficulty in observing these physical traits which so distinguish the Canary people such as, according to Dr. Schwidetzky: their broad, short faces; prominent cheekbones; sharp chin; small noses, broad rather than long and more concave than convex; deep-set eyes sloping upwards; curved, rather than straight, eyebrows; lighter eyes and darker hair; a greater profusion of fingerprints... Some less important features are: wide mouths; thick lips; large, very lively eyes; large, white teeth.

Some of the most distinguished researchers and anthropologists to have studied the ancient Guanches have been R. Verneau, S. Berthelot, Fischer in 1930, Fuste in 1959, Rösing in 1967 and a special mention must be made of Dr. Isle Schwidestzky in 1963 and 1975. They have declared that the ancient race of the Guanches still exists today and that a comparison of Guanche skulls with those of present-day Canary Islanders shows a great similarity.

In Tenerife, according to Wölfel in 1930, «... the Spanish immigration could be calculated at a third of the present population»[111].

If we base evidence, firstly, on historical sources that until only a short while ago were concealed from us and, secondly, on statistics produced by anthropologists in recent years, we can prove conclusively that the guanches are still the dominant race in the Canary Islands.

The guanches live on in the presentday Canary Islanders!

In common with so many other traditions, the stick game has lasted through the centuries, passed on from father to son. The Verga family of La Esperanza in Tenerife show us how the game is still practised as in former times.

In the faces of these people can be seen the features of the Guanches in the present day, although they are not necessarily the most representative of their race nor the purest.

The whistling in La Gomera is a Guanche language which has survived until present times. The Gomeros communicate with this language over long distances.

These men from La Palma still follow the Guanche tradition of using poles to help them vault over cliffs and gullies. This custom has survived on other islands, too.

EPILOGUE

Many years have passed since I wrote this book, as I reread it now I feel the same about everything I said then; nor do I regret the simple style I used, although I admit that some paragraphs could be bettered from the literary point of view. But in the form used in 1982 the book became the most accepted one in the Canary Islands and had an equal success in its English and German translations. I owe gratitude and respect to all those readers. Since the subject of the Guanches is so complex I had to use a certain amount of quotations from texts written by various authors; I found that system to be more honest than incorporating their statements and present them as something of my own.

The theory of the Guanches, as presented here, has developed favourably in the last years. Doubts have been removed and, most important, it has been accepted that the Guanche race as such did not disapeared. Even more positive: there never was a Guanche minority as opposed to the alien population. All this does not mean that there are not some interested parties left who still continue to confuse the issue with supposedly true dates or try to distort the reality of facts.

The reader has the opportunity of visiting the *Museo Canario* in Las Palmas (Gran Canaria) or the *Museo Arqueológico* in Santa Cruz de Tenerife. There the physic constitution of the aborigines can be verified and it can be observed that there was nothing surprising in their appearance as their facial traits are still to be found among the Canarian populations of today in spite of the logical evolution through the radical changes which came about after the submission. We also must bear in mind that the Canarian peasants who emigrated to the American continent were included in the books registering the half-breed *(mes-tizos)* of those countries since they looked like them.

Archaeological investigations during these last years have contributed to elucidate certain significant aspects. It has been proved that there have been human settlements on the islands as far back as six hundred years before Christ. Majorcans who arrived in the mid 13th century in Gran Canaria settled on some ruins of dwellings built of stone according to the methods of that island. Moreover, these houses were already equipped with wooden doors, according to previous reports.

The depth studies of anthropology carried out by Dr. Ilse Schwidetzky in the sixties and seventies of the twentieth century and published by the *Cabildo* of Tenerife have revealed what can be called revolutionary scientific facts in regard to physical traits and blood groups of present day's Canarians which coincide on a large scale with those of the Guanches. Another subject is the classification which this researcher has made relating to the Cromagnon and mediterranean types; she may have been mistaken in this aspect but it that does not invalidate the rest of her work.

Some authors have underrated in an inconceivable way the culture of the Guanches. If we analyze the virtues and the knowledge of our ancestors who lived isolated and had no access to metals we have to conclude that these were civilized people of whom one could learn and make use of many things. To illustrate some of this, I add photos which may help the readers to reach their own conclusions.

Stone mill (Museo Arqueológico de Santa Cruz de Tenerife).

Bowl from Gran Canaria (Museo Canario).

Tofio, bowl for milking - from Fuerteventura (Museo Canario, Las Palmas).

Wooden bowl from La Gomera
(Museo Arqueológico de Santa Cruz de Tenerife).

Ceramic receptacle - from Gran Canaria (Museo Canario, Las Palmas).

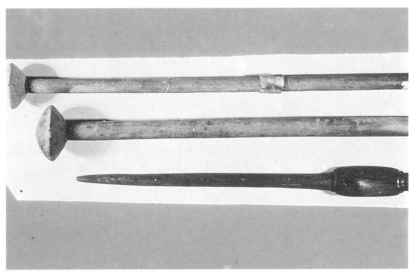

(Añepas) Batons, signs of authority and a (banot) weapon.
(Museo Arqueológico de Santa Cruz de Tenerife).

Artistic seal made of ceramic (Museo Canario, Las Palmas).

Artistic seal made of ceramic (Museo Canario, Las Palmas).

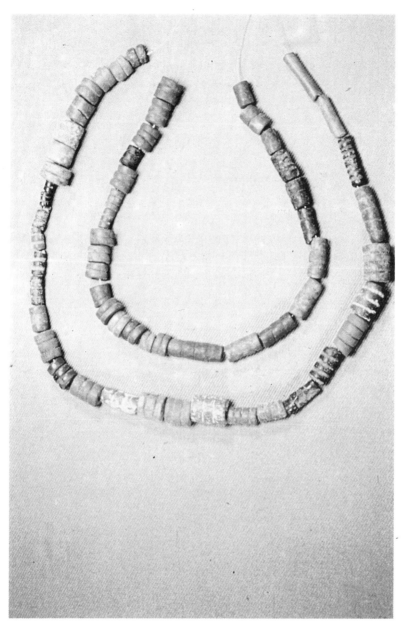

Necklace of clay beads (Museo Arqueológico de Santa Cruz de Tenerife).

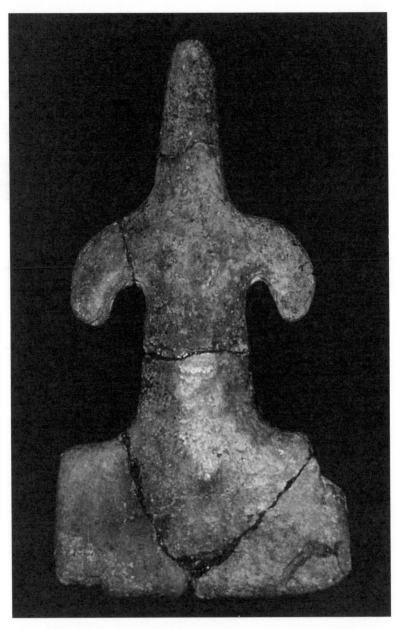

Antropomorphic feminine figure (Museo Canario, Las Palmas).

Bag made of goat leather (Museo Canario, Las Palmas).

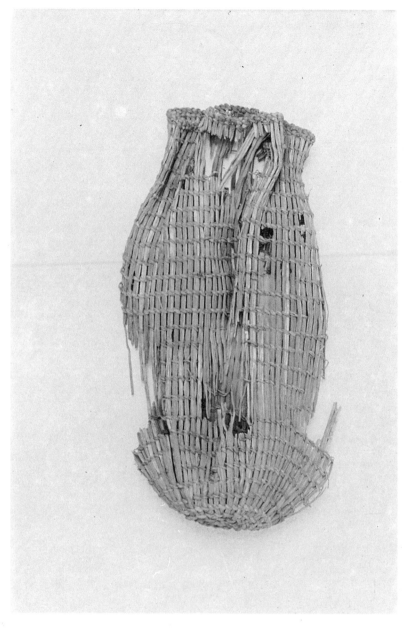

Bag made of reed (Museo Canario, Las Palmas).

Phehistoric rock carving (Cueva de Belmaco, Mazo, La Palma).

Prehistoric village, zonzamas, Lanzarote.

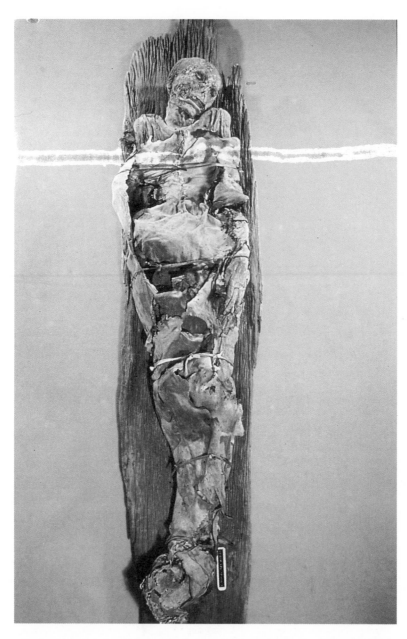

Guanche mummy (Museo Arqueológico de Santa Cruz de Tenerife).

NOTES

(1) Abreu Galindo, «Historia de la Conquista de las siete islas Canarias», pp. 49, 87, 149 and 291.
(2) Schwidetzky, «La Poblacion Prehispánica e Investigaciones Antropológicas en las Islas Canarias». Archaeological Museum, S/C. de Tenerife, 1663 and 1975.
(3) Schwidetzky, above-mentioned work.
(4) «Le Canarien», Chap. LVIII.
(5) Espinosa, «Historia de Nuestra Señora de Candelaria», p. 42.
(6) Morales Padrón, F. (A. Sedeño), 1978, p. 371.
(7) Torriani, «Descripción de las Islas Canarias», pp. 107-108.
(8) Espinosa, above-mentioned work, p. 37.
(9) A. Galindo, above-mentioned work, pp. 159 and 269 and Espinosa, above-mentioned work, p. 38.
(10) Espinosa, above-mentioned work, p. 38.
(11) A. Galindo, above-mentioned work, p. 149.
(12) A. Galindo, above-mentioned work, p. 157.
(13) Siemens Hernández, «La Música en Canarias», p. 27.
(14) A. Galindo, above-mentioned work, p.155.
(15) A. Galindo, above-mentioned work, p. 156.
(16) Espinosa, above-mentioned work, p. 46.
(17) A. Galindo, above-mentioned work, p. 266.
(18) A. Galindo, above-mentioned work, pp. 31-32.
(19) Espinosa, above-mentioned work, p. 32.
(20) Sabino Berthelot, «Etnografía y Anales de la Conquista de las Islas Canarias», Goya Ediciones, 1978, pp. 150, 151, 152, 158 and 159.
(21) González Antón, R. and Tejera Gaspar, A. «Los Aborígenes Canarios», p. 172.
(22) González Antón, R. and Tejera Gaspar, A., above-mentioned work, p. 204.
(23) «Le Canarien», p. 134.

(24) Millares Torres A. «Historia General de las Islas Canarias», Las Palmas de Gran Canaria, 1975. Vol. II, p. 53.
(25) «Le Canarien», p. 43.
(26) «Le Canarien», p. 84.
(27) A. Galindo, above-mentioned work, pp. 80-81.
(28) A. Galindo, above-mentioned work, p. 182.
(29) A. Galindo, above-metnioned work, p. 182.
(30) Morales Padrón, Gómez Escudero, «Historia de la Conquista de Gran Canaria», 1978, p. 57.
(31) A. Galindo, pp. 199 and 204.
(32) Millares Torres, A., Above-Mentioned work, Vol. II, p. 179.
    A. Galindo, p. 211.
(33) A. Galindo, above-mentioned work, p. 214.
(34) A. Galindo, above-mentioned work, p. 214.
(35) A. Galindo, above-metnioned work, p. 228.
(36) A. Galindo, above-mentioned work, p. 231.
(37) A. Galindo, p. 234.
(38) A. Galindo, above-mentioned work, pp. 267-268.
(39) A. Galindo, above-mentioned work, p. 278.
(40) A. Galindo, above-mentioned work, p. 286.
(41) Espinosa, above-mentioned,work, p. 96.
(42) Rumeu de Armas, A. «La Conquista de Tenerife», p. 186.
(43) Rumeu de Armas, A., above-mentioned work, p. 254.
(44) Espinosa, above-mentioned work, p. 109.
(45) Espinosa, above-mentioned work, pp. 96-97.
(46) Rumeu de Armas, A., «La Política Indigenista de Isabel la Católica», pp. 29 and 30.
(47) Rumeu de Armas, A., above-mentioned work, p. 82.
(48) Rumeu de Armas, A., above-mentioned work, pp. 87 and 88.
(49) Rumeu de Armas, A., above-mentioned work, pp. 94 and 95.
(50) Serra Rafols and Leopoldo de la Rosa, «Fontes Refum Canariarum IV», p. 68.
(51) Serra Rafols and Leopoldo de la Rosa, above-mentioned work, p. 27.
(52) Serra Rafols and Leopoldo de la Rosa, above-mentioned work, p. 27.
(53) Serra Rafols and Leopoldo de la Rosa, above-mentioned work, p. 92.
(54) Rumeu de Armas, «La Política Indigenista de Isabel la Católica», p. 62.
(55) Millares Torres, A., above-mentioned work, Vol. III, p. 127.
(56) Wolfel, D., «La Curia Romana y la Corona de España en defensa de los aborígenes canarios», p. 1.062.
(57) A. Galindo, p. 239.
(58) A. Galindo, pp. 179, 224, 226 and 227.
(59) A. Galindo, p. 231.
(60) Rumeu de Armas, «La política Indigenista de Isabel la Católica», p. 288.
(61) Jiménez Sánchez, S., «Primer repartimiento de tierra y agua de Gran Canaria», 1939.
(62) A. Galindo, p. 325.
(63) Serra Rafols, Elías. «Las Datas de Tenerife», 1978.
(64) Wolfel, above-mentioned work, pp. 1.058 and 1.060.
(65) Wolfel, above-mentioned work, pp. 1.020 and 1.051.
(66) Wolfel, above-mentioned work, pp. 1.022, 1.061 and 1.062.
(67) Rumeu de Armas, «La Política Indigenista de Isabel la Católica», p. 61.
(68) Rumeu de Armas, above-mentioned work, p. 70.
(69) Rumeu de Armas, «La Política Indigenista de Isabel la Católica», pp. 88-89.
(70) Rumeu de Armas, above-mentioned work, p. 90.
(71) Rumeu de Armas, above-mentioned work, p. 92.
(72) Rumeu de Armas, above-mentioned work, p. 93.
(73) Rumeu de Armas, above-mentioned work, p. 94-95.
(74) Rumeu de Armas, above-mentioned work, p. 107.

(75) Rumeu de Armas, «La Política Indigenista de Isable la Católica», p. 111.
(76) Rumeu de Armas, «La Política Indigenista de Isabel la Católica», p. 97.
(77) Rumeu de Armas, above-mentioned work, p. 97.
(78) Rumeu de Armas, above-mentioned work, p. 97.
(79) Fontes Rerum Canariarum IV, p. 92.
(80) Rumeu de Armas, above-mentioned work, p. 97.
(81) Rumeu de Armas, «La Política Indigenista de Isabel la Católica», p. 62.
(82) Manuel Marrero, «La esclavitud en Tenerife a través de la conquista», p. 82.
(83) Manuela Marrero, «La esclavitud en Tenerife a través de la conquista», pp. 88-89.
(84) Manuela Marrero, above-mentioned work, p. 104.
(85) Manuela Marrero, «La esclavitud en Tenerife a través de la conquista», p. 101.
(86) Manuela Marrero, above-mentioned work, pp. 102, 103 and 104.
(87) Millares Torres A., «Historia General de las Islas Canarias», Vol. III, p. 190.
(88) Millares Torres A., «Historia General de las Islas Canarias», Vol. III, pp. 190-191.
(89) Espinosa, above-mentioned work, p. 45.
(90) Millares Torres, A. «Historia General de las Islas Canarias», Vol. III, p. 130.
(91) Espinosa, above-mentioned work, p. 125.
(92) Victor Grau Basas, «Usos y costumbres de la población campesina de Gran Canaria» (1855-1888), p. 13.
(93) Victor Grau Basas, above-mentioned work, p. 17.
(94) Victor Grau Basas, above-mentioned work, p. 17.
(95) Victor Grau Basas, above-mentioned work, p. 17.
(96) Victor Grau Basas, above-mentioned work, p. 29.
(97) Verneau, «Cinco años de estancia en las Islas Canarias», p. 157.
(98) Verneau, above-mentioned work, pp. 204-205.
(99) Verneau, above-mentioned work, pp. 218.
(100) Verneau, above-mentioned work, p. 226.
(101) Verneau, above-mentioned work, p. 234.
(102) Verneau, above-mentioned work, p. 172.
(103) Verneau, above-mentioned work, p. 238.
(104) Diego Cuscoy, «Los guanches», p. 223.
(105) Diego Cuscoy, «Los guanches», p. 223.
(106) Diego Cuscoy, «Los guanches», p. 224.
(107) Millares Torres, A., «Historia General de las Islas Canarias», Vol. III, p. 127.
(108) Millares Torres, A., above-mentioned work, p. 127.
(109) Rumeu de Armas, «La conquista de Tenerife», p. 115.
(110) Ilse Schwidetzky, «Investigaciones antropológicas in the Canary Islands», 1975. p. 92.
(111) Schwidetzky, «Investigaciones antropológicas en las Islas Canarias», 1975, p. 73.

BIBLIOGRAPHY

-ABREU GALINDO, J. "Historia general de las Siete Islas Canarias". Goya Ediciones, S/C de Tenerife, 1977.

-ALMAGRO, M. "El arte rupestre del Africa del Norte en relación con la rama norteafricana de Cro-Magnon". Anuario de Estudios Atlánticos, Madrid, 1969.

-ALONSO, M.R. "El poema de Viana", Madrid, 1952.

-ALVAREZ DELGADO, J. "La conquista de Tenerife. Un reajuste de datos hasta 1496". Revista de Historia. La Laguna de Tenerife.

"Los aborígenes canarios ante la lingüística". Atlantis, Madrid, 1941.

"Inscripciones líbicas de Canarias. Ensayos de interpretación". La Laguna, 1964.

"Analogías Arqueológicas canario-africanas". Revista de Historia Canaria, 1967.

-ANUARIO DE ESTUDIOS ATLANTICO I, 1955.

-AZURARA, G. "Crónica do descobrimiento e conquista de Guiné". Edición Carreira-Santaren, Paris, 1841.

-BERTHELOT, S. "Etnografía y anales de la conquista de las Islas Canarias". Goya Ediciones. S/C de Tenerife, 1978.

-BLANCO MONTESDEOCA, J. "Breve noticia histórica de las Islas Canarias". Edición 1976. Excmo. Cabildo Insular de G. Canaria.

-BONTIER Y LE VERRIER. "Le Canarien". Instituto de Estudios Canarios. La Laguna - Las Palmas, 1960.

-BOSCH MILLARES, J. "La medicina canaria en la época prehispánica". Anuario de Estudios Atlánticos, 1962. Madrid - Las Palmas.

"Paleopatología ósea de los primitivos pobladores de Canarias". Cabildo Insular de G. Canaria, 1975.

-BRAVO, T. "Geografía de Canarias". Goya Ediciones, S/C de Tenerife, 1954.

-CIORANESCU, A. "Historia de Santa Cruz de Tenerife". Servicio de Publicaciones de la Caja General de Ahorros de S/C de Tenerife, 1977.

"Juan de Bethencourt". Aula de Cultura de Tenerife, 1982.

-COELLO GOMEZ - RODRIGUEZ GONZALEZ - PARRILLA LOPEZ. "Protocolos de Alonso Gutiérrez" (1522-1525). Aula de Cultura del Cabildo Insular de Tenerife, en colaboración con el Instituto de Estudios Canarios. S/C de Tenerife, 1980.

-CORTES, V. "La conquista de las Islas Canarias a través de la venta de esclavos en Valencia". Anuario de Estudios Atlánticos, 1955.

-CHIL Y NARANJO. "Estudios históricos, climatológicos y fitopatológicos de las Islas Canarias". Las Palmas de G. Canaria, 1876.

-DARIAS Y PADRON. "Historia de la religión en Canarias". Editorial Cervantes, S/C de Tenerife, 1957.

-DEL ARCO AGUILAR, C. "El enterramiento canario prehispánico". Complemento de la Historia General de Canarias de Agustín Millares Torres, 1975.

-DE LA ROSA OLIVERA, I. "Vecindario de la Ciudad de S. Cristóbal de La Laguna en el s. XVI". La Laguna, 1949.

"Notas sobre los Reyes de Tenerife y sus familias". Revista de Historia. La Laguna de Tenerife.

-DE LA ROSA OLIVERA Y SERRA RAFOLS. "Acuerdos del Cabildo de Tenerife" (1508-1513). Fontes Rerum Canariarum V. La Laguna de Tenerife, 1952.

"Acuerdos del Cabildo de Tenerife" (1514-1518). Fontes Rerum Canariarum XII. La Laguna de Tenerife, 1965.

"El Adelantado D. Alonso de Lugo y su Residencia por Lope de Sosa". Fontes Rerum Canariarum III. La Laguna de Tenerife, 1949.

"Proceso de Reformación del Repartimiento de Tenerife". Fontes Rerum Canariarum VI. La Laguna de Tenerife, 1953.

-DIEGO CUSCOY, L. "Armas de los primitivos canarios". Aula de Cultura del Cabildo de Tenerife, 1968.

"Los Guanches". Museo Arqueológico, S/C de Tenerife, 1968.

"Los molinos de mano". Revista de Historia, La Laguna de Tenerife, 1950.

"Notas para una historia de la antropología canaria". Complemento de la Historia General de Canarias de Agustín Millares Torres, 1975.

-ESPINOSA, A. "Historia de Nuestra Sra. de Candelaria". Goya Ediciones, S/C de Tenerife, 1967.

"Fontes Rerum Canariarum". Instituto de Estudios Canarios. El Museo Canario. La Laguna - Las Palmas, 1959. (Varios tomos).

-FUSTE ARA, M. "Algunas observaciones acerca de la antropología de las poblaciones prehispánicas actuales de G. Canaria". Revista El Museo Canario, 1958-1959.

-GARCIA MARQUEZ, F. "Almogarens y Goros" Una construcción aborígen en la montaña de Tauro. (G. Canaria). Anuario de Estudios Atlánticos, 1968.

-GOMEZ ESCUDERO, P. "Historia de la conquista de G. Canaria". El Museo Canario, 1978.

-GONZALEZ ANTON, R. - TEJERA GASPAR, A. "Los aborígenes canarios". Secretariado de publicaciones Universidad de La Laguna, 1981.

-GONZALEZ YANES Y MARRERO RODRIGUEZ. Protocolos de Hernán Guerra". Fontes Rerum Canariarum VII, La Laguna de Tenerife, 1958.

-GUERRA CABRERA, P. "Los guanches del Sur de Tenerife". Colección de Historia del Centro de la Cultura Popular Canaria (CCPC). La Laguna, 1980.

-GRAU BASSAS, V. "Usos y costumbres de la población campesina de Gran Canaria" (1885 - 1888). El Museo Canario, 1980.

-HERNANDEZ GARCIA, J. "Algunos aspectos de la emigración de las Islas Canarias a Hispanoamérica en la segunda mitad del S. XIX" (1840-1895). Bohlau Verlag, 1976.

-HERNANDEZ PEREZ, M. "Contribución a la carta arqueológica de la Isla de La Palma". Anuario de Estudios Atlánticos. Madrid, 1972.

"Pinturas y grabados rupestres en el Archipiélago Canario". Complemento de la Historia General de Canarias de Agustín Millares Torres, 1975.

-JIMENEZ DE GREGORIO. "La población de las Islas Canarias en la segunda mitad del s. XVIII". Anuario de Estudios Atlánticos.

-JIMENEZ SANCHEZ, S. "La prehistoria de G. Canaria". Revista de Historia, La Laguna, 1945.

-LADERO, M.A. "Estructura económica de Canarias a comienzos del s. XVI". Revista Campus, Nº 0.

-LOPEZ HERRERA, S. "Las Islas Canarias a través de la Historia". Madrid, 1972.

-MARIN Y CUBAS, T. "Historia de las Siete Islas Canarias". 1964.

-MARTIN SOCAS, D. "Etnología aborígen de Lanzarote y Fuerteventura". Complemento de la Historia General de Canarias de Agustín Millares Torres, 1975.

-MARRERO RODRIGUEZ, M. "Protocolos del escribano Juan Ruiz de Berlànga". Fontes Rerum Canariarum XVIII. La Laguna de Tenerife, 1974.

"La esclavitud en Tenerife a raiz de la conquista". Instituto de Estudios Canarios. La Laguna de Tenerife, 1966.

-MILLARES TORRES, A. "Historia General de las Islas Canarias". Complementada con elaboraciones actuales de diversos especialistas. Las Palmas de G. Canaria, 1975. Tomos I, II y III.

"Historia de la inquisición en las Islas Canarias". Anuario de estudios medievales. Editorial Benchomo 1981.

-MORALES PADRON, F. "Canarias en América y América en Canarias". Revista de Estudios Americanos. Sevilla, 1956.

-NATURA Y CULTURA DE LAS ISLAS CANARIAS. S/C de Tenerife, 1979. Tercera Edición.

-NAVARRO ARTILES, F. "Teberite, diccionario de la lengua aborígen canaria". Las Palmas de Gran Canaria, 1981.

-NUÑEZ DE LA PEÑA, J. "Conquista y antigüedades de las islas de la Gran Canaria...". Santa Cruz de Tenerife, 1847.

-PERAZA DE AYALA, J. "Juan de las Casas y el Señorío de Canarias". Revista de Historia. La Laguna de Tenerife.

"El Régimen comercial de Canarias con las Indias en los s. XVI, XVII y XVIII". Universidad de La Laguna. Facultad de Filosofía y Letras, 1952.

-PEREZ VOITURIEZ. "Problemas jurídicos-internacionales de la conquista de Canarias". Universidad de La Laguna. Secretariado de Publicaciones, 1958.

-PEREZ DE BORRADAS, J. "Estado actual de las investigaciones prehistóricas sobre Canarias". Las Palmas de G. Canaria, 1939. El Museo Canario.

-RUMEU DE ARMAS, A. "Alonso de Lugo en la Corte de los Reyes Católicos". Biblioteca Reyes Católicos. Madrid, 1952.

"La política indigenista de Isabel la Católica". Instituto Isabel la Católica de Historia Eclesiástica, Valladolid, 1969.

"La Conquista de Tenerife". Aula de Cultura de Tenerife, 1975.

"Piratería y ataques navales contra las Islas Canarias". C.S.I.C., Madrid, 1945.

-SCHWIDETZKY, I. "La población prehispánica de las Islas Canarias". Museo Arqueológico. S/C de Tenerife, 1963.

"Investigaciones antropológicas en las Islas Canarias". Museo Arqueológico, S/C de Tenerife, 1975.

-SEDEÑO, A. "Historia de la conquista de G. Canaria". Galdar, 1936.

-SERRA RAFOLS, E. "La Arqueología Canaria". La Laguna de Tenerife, 1918.

"La navegación primitiva en los mares de Canarias". Revista de Historia, La Laguna, 1957.

"El Adelantado Alonso de Lugo". A. C. de Tenerife.

"I Redescubrimiento de las Islas Canarias en el s. XIV". La Laguna de Tenerife, 1961.

"Acuerdos del Cabildo de Tenerife" (1497-1508). Fontes Rerum Canariarum IV. La Laguna de Tenerife, 1949.

"Los portugueses en Canarias". Discurso inaugural en la Universidad de S. Fernando de La Laguna, 1941-42.

"Las Datas de Tenerife". Instituto de Estudios Canarios. La Laguna de Tenerife, 1978.

-SERRA RAFOLS Y DE LA ROSA OLIVERA. "Los reinos de Tenerife". La Laguna, 1945.

"Acuerdos del Cabildo de Tenerife" (1497-1507) - (1508-1513) - (1514-1518) - (1518-1525). Colección Fontes Rerum Canariarum, I.C.E.

–SIEMENS HERNANDEZ, L.: «La música en Canarias». El Museo Canario. Las Palmas de Gran Canaria, 1977.

«La música aborigen». Complemento a la Historia General de Canarias de Agustín Millares Torres, 1975.

los aborígenes canarios», Anthropos XXV. Viena, 1930.

«Los esclavos guanches en la isla de Madeira». Periódico La Provincia. Las Palmas de Gran Canaria, 12-VIII-1983,

–TORRIANI, L.: «Descripción de las Islas Canarias» Ed. Goya, S/C de Tenerife, 1959.

–TRUJILLO CABRERA, J.: «Episodios gomeros del siglo XV». Ed. Gráficas de Tenerife, 1969.

–VERNEAU, R.: «Cinco años de estancia en las islas Canarias». Ediciones J.A.D.L. La Orotava, Tenerife, 1981.

–VIANA, A. «Antigüedades de las Islas Afortunadas de la Gran Canaria», La Laguna, 1968.

«Conquista de Tenerife y aparescimiento de la ymagen de Candelaria». Edición por Alejandro Cioranescu. Aula de Cultura de Tenerife, 1968.

–VIERA Y CLAVIJO, J: «Noticias de la Historia General de las Islas Canarias». Goya Ediciones, S/C de Tenerife, 1967, Sexta Edición.

–YANES CARRILLO, A.: «Cosas viejas de la mar». J. Régulo, Editor, S/C de La Palma, 1953.

–WÖLFEL. «Un jefe de la tribu gomera y sus relaciones con con la Curia Romana». Investigación y Progreso. Madrid, 1930.

"La Curia Romana y la Corona de España en la defensa de los aborígenes canarios". Anthropos XXV. Viena, 1930.

BIOGRAPHY

José Luis Concepción was born in Breña Alta (La Palma), Canary Islands, on 15th April, 1948. After he left school, he studied music and later joined his local town band. In the evenings he studied for his advanced school examinations whilst going out to work during the day.

At eighteen years of age he left for England and remained there for ten years, during which time he studied English and other languages, working in the hotel business and as an insurance salesman.

He returned to the Canary Islands when he was twenty-eight and taugh English in a private school, then later worked as a tourist guide. In 1979 he started up his own small, construction firm, combining his work with history studies. Since then, he has written a good number of books relating to history, geography, nature and traditions, including a dictionary. He has also two other books translated into English and German: **Typical canary cooking** and **Nature and History of the Canary Islands**.

In 1984 he founded the *Asociación Cultural de las Islas Canarias* (Canary Islands Cultural Asociation) to promote cultural activities, and from 1986 to 1989 he had a weekly radio programme broadcasting to the Canary Islands.

In 1988 he began to study geography and history at university and finished the speciality in history in 1991. From 1993 to 1995 he went again to university and carried out the studies for two doctorships: history and sociology.